Mercy Triumphs, Grace Abounds

Pamela Ramsey

authorHOUSE®

AuthorHouse™
1663 Liberty Drive
Bloomington, IN 47403
www.authorhouse.com
Phone: 1-800-839-8640

Published by AuthorHouse 8/7/2012

ISBN: 978-1-4685-5434-2 (e)
ISBN: 978-1-4685-5435-9 (sc)

Library of Congress Control Number: 2012903158

The front cover was designed by Julia DeHart Hudson (2011), and depicts a tear jar. Psalm 56:8
(NKJV) "You number my wanderings; Put my tears into Your bottle; Are they not in Your book?"

"...judgment without mercy will be shown to anyone who has not been merciful. Mercy triumphs over judgment!"
(James 2:13)

"Moreover the law entered that the offense might abound. But where sin abounded, grace abounded much more, so that as sin reigned in death, even so grace might reign through righteousness to eternal life through Jesus Christ our Lord."
(Romans 5:20-21)

ACKNOWLEDGMENTS

I want to express my deep appreciation for Dr. David Powlison and Peggy Sterling who have been my "encouragers" while writing this workbook. Early on they read the manuscript and offered indispensable advice. Peggy has typed every word into the computer and been a fastidious copy editor. Also, my thanks goes to Kim Baker and Julie Crane who helped me refine the workbook and added questions for group discussion. My greatest praise and thanks go to my great God and Savior for motivating me to write this and allowing me the privilege of participating in His healing of post-abortive women.

I dedicate this workbook to my post-abortive sisters with the prayer that it will be an instrument of healing in God's hands.
Amen.

Mercy Triumphs, Grace Abounds!
Table of Contents

INTRODUCTION

Greetings to you, dear sister, as you begin this Bible study. I am excited that God has initiated and will continue to do a wonderful work in you! My prayer is that this post-abortion Bible study and workbook will be a helpful tool used by our awesome, loving and forgiving God to bring healing in your life.

This study was designed primarily for post-abortive women who are believers. If you are unsure as to whether you are a believer in Jesus Christ or even what is meant by that term, please read the short explanation on page 89. As a believer, you have the Holy Spirit indwelling you and working in your heart. Even with the Spirit's help, abortion is a very painful and difficult issue to address. I hope you share my conviction that God's word is all-sufficient and that it does offer truth and hope for healing. The Holy Spirit is able to give you the desire to be transformed, the comfort you need and the illumination of God's truth as you proceed on this healing journey.

What do I mean by healing? Healing is a metaphor for the reality that God through Jesus Christ can touch and change you in all aspects of your life. God heals in the sense that your relationship with Him will become closer and more precious. Also, broken relationships with other people will be reconciled and improved. Physical healing from abortion's effects is also in view, whether the healing takes place now or in the resurrection. Healing also refers to God's comfort for the myriad of troubling emotions you may feel (i.e. guilt, shame, depression, anger, sorrow, fear, self-pity, etc.) Somehow, in His great mercy and grace He removes the power and sting of the intense feelings that surround an abortion. The Lord can help you rethink your past so you replace destructive thought patterns with biblical understanding. And healing also refers to the growing desire you'll have to be obedient to Him and to change your lifestyle choices and habits so you live worthy of His calling.

I know from my own personal experience that God can heal. When I was 26 years old and beginning my first job as a teacher, I was absolutely taken by surprise to find that I was pregnant. My boyfriend was never given a part of the decision; I called him up and told him I was having an abortion. And I did! And then I experienced the fruits of that choice which included deep depression especially around the anniversary date of the abortion, trouble trusting men, anger at my boyfriend and other effects which are now called "post abortion syndrome." You may have experienced these and/or others. But that's not the end of my story! I can also say, rejoicing, that God healed me and redeemed my past beyond what I ever imagined! He can do the same for you as He did for me. Jesus Christ is the same yesterday, today, and forever–for every woman, in every situation, in every place. He knows you and extends His mercy and healing touch to you also.

You are setting out on an exciting adventure with God! Keep the goal in sight–a warm, deep, personal relationship with God and all the joy, peace and hope that result will be yours! Although God ultimately brings about the changes, you are called to step out in faith and in submission to His working. Opening up old wounds can be very difficult and painful. I remember when I was asked to participate in a post-abortion healing group. I thought I had worked through my abortion and had been pretty much "healed." So I was surprised by the intensity of the anger and resistance I experienced as I anticipated the first session of the group. My encouragement to you, at the very outset, is to persevere even when it is tough emotionally. Be assured that God is able and willing to heal you! It may not seem possible now, but someday you will share the psalmist's testimony *"O Lord my God, I called to you for help and you healed me." Psalm 30:2*

The format of the workbook includes reading Scriptures, answering questions by observing the text and reflecting upon and praying God's truth. I would highly recommend that you take the time to actually write answers to the questions, either in the spaces provided or separately. I think you'll find that the process of writing will help you clarify your thoughts and feelings. Each chapter has readings for five days and ideally you should spend 15-30 minutes to thoroughly process one day's reading and answering of questions. You will notice that in addition to the asterisked (*) questions for each day's reading, there are also questions marked with a heart symbol (♥) representing personal questions, and a key (⚷) symbol, representing key questions. Questions introduced by either the heart or key symbols will be your discussion questions for doing the study *within a group setting*. But please answer all of the questions whether you are involved with a group or whether you are doing the book as an individual. They are all designed to help you with your healing journey. Interspersed between chapters are testimonies from post-abortive women to flesh out the reality that God does heal!

Chapter One:
GOD IS ABLE TO HEAL

Who is God? Does He really have the ability and power to touch your life and change you? The world around us and maybe even your own life seems out of control. Is God really sovereign with absolute authority and power over every person and event? Even including you and your abortion(s)? This chapter is meant to deepen your trust in God by focusing on Scriptures which highlight His ability. He is able to heal!

Day 1
Scripture: Exodus 15:22-26
"Then Moses led Israel from the Red Sea and they went into the Desert of Shur. For three days they traveled in the desert without finding water. When they came to Marah, they could not drink its water because it was bitter. (That is why the place is called Marah.) So the people grumbled against Moses, saying, 'What are we to drink?' Then Moses cried out to the Lord, and the Lord showed him a piece of wood. He threw it into the water, and the water became sweet. There the Lord made a decree and a law for them, and there He tested them. He said, 'If you listen carefully to the voice of the Lord your God and do what is right in His eyes, if you pay attention to His commands and keep all His decrees, I will not bring on you any of the diseases I brought on the Egyptians, for I am the Lord who heals you.' "

* What was the problem faced by the Israelites?

* What did Moses do to solve the problem?

* How did God identify Himself?

❤ When you are in a spiritually dry place, what can God provide?

Scripture: Psalm 103:1-5

      "Praise the Lord, O my soul; all my inmost being, praise His holy name. Praise the Lord, O my soul, and forget not all His benefits. He forgives all my sins and heals all my diseases; He redeems my life from the pit and crowns me with love and compassion. He satisfies my desires with good things, so that my youth is renewed like the eagle's."

* Who is the One who forgives, heals, redeems, crowns and satisfies?

Scripture: Isaiah 53:5

      "But He was pierced for our transgressions, He was crushed for our iniquities; the punishment that brought us peace was upon Him, and by His wounds we are healed."

* The "He" in this passage is Christ. It says we are healed by His wounds. What caused Christ's wounds?

‽ All three of today's Scripture passages state that the Lord heals. Besides physical healing, what other types of healing could be in view?

Day 2

Scripture: Isaiah 61:1-3

      1"The Spirit of the Sovereign Lord is on me, because the Lord has anointed me to preach good news to the poor. He has sent me to bind up the brokenhearted, to proclaim freedom for the captives and release for the prisoners, 2 to proclaim the year of the Lord's favor and the day of vengeance of our God, to comfort all who mourn, 3 and provide for those who grieve in Zion—to bestow on them a crown of beauty instead of ashes, the oil of gladness instead of mourning, and a garment of praise instead of a spirit of despair. They will be called oaks of righteousness, a planting of the Lord for the display of his splendor."

* Make a list of all the things in verses 1&2 which the "Anointed One" is to do. Include the verb, object of the verb and recipient(s) of the action.

For example, in verse 1, preach (verb) good news (object) to poor (recipients).

* Circle the phrases listed above which you identify with or desire.

❧ He promises to exchange three things in verse 3. Write out these exchanges:

* What's the ultimate result of these exchanges?

♥ In what ways does your spirit of despair (verse 3) reveal itself?

Please observe that the actions of the "Anointed One" are wide-ranging and benefit the recipients. His work in their lives displays the Lord's splendor. This truth applied to us means that God shows His glory and amazing power by His work in our lives.

Scripture: Luke 4:16-21

"He went to Nazareth, where He had been brought up, and on the Sabbath day He went into the synagogue, as was His custom. And He stood up to read. The scroll of the prophet Isaiah was handed to Him. Unrolling it, He found the place where it is written: 'The Spirit of the Lord is on me, because He has anointed me to preach good news to the poor. He has sent me to heal the broken hearted. He has sent me to proclaim freedom for the prisoners and recovery of sight for the blind, to release the oppressed, to proclaim the year of the Lord's favor.' Then He rolled up the scroll, gave it back to the attendant and sat down. The eyes of everyone in the synagogue were fastened on Him, and He said to them, 'Today this Scripture is fulfilled in your hearing.' "

* Who does Christ imply is the "Anointed One" referred to in Isaiah 61 on the previous page?

* Read Isaiah 61:1-3 again. Write out a prayer to Christ in response to this passage. Ask Him to do anything mentioned in these verses for you personally. Read it aloud to Him.

Day 3

Scripture: Gen 18:14

"Is anything too hard for the Lord? I will return to you at the appointed time next year and Sarah will have a son."

* What does God say isn't too hard for Him?

Scripture: Jeremiah 32:17; 26-27

"Ah, Sovereign Lord, you have made the heavens and the earth by your great power and outstretched arm. Nothing is too hard for you...
Then the word of the Lord came to Jeremiah: I am the Lord, the God of all mankind. Is anything too hard for me?"

* On what fact does Jeremiah base his assessment of God's ability?

❤ Based on these verses, is healing you too difficult for God?

⊷ What do you believe about God's power to do absolutely anything?

Scripture: Job 42:2 (Job speaking to God)

"I know that you can do all things; no plan of yours can be thwarted."

* Say Job's confession out loud to God.

* Write out any doubts that you have regarding God's ability or power:

Day 4

Scripture: Matthew 9:20-22.

"Just then a woman who had been subject to bleeding for twelve years came up behind Him and touched the edge of His cloak. She said to herself, If I only touch His cloak, I will be healed. Jesus turned and saw her. 'Take heart, daughter,' He said, 'your faith has healed you.' And the woman was healed from that moment."

* Briefly recount the incident.

* What did she believe?

* Who or what was the object of her faith?

* What exactly made the woman well? her faith literally? or the object of her faith?

The Greek word that is translated "healed" here comes from a verb which can also mean "to save" or "to be made whole."

☙ In this instance, do you think Jesus is just talking about physical healing when He says her faith has healed her?

Scripture: Matthew 14:35b-36
"People brought all their sick to Him and begged Him to let the sick just touch the edge of His cloak, and all who touched Him were healed."

* What happened to people when they touched Jesus?

* In verse 36, the word translated "healed" is a stronger version of the Greek verb used in the previous passage. It means to be made perfectly whole or to be completely restored to health. Jesus is able to heal you completely–physically, emotionally, mentally and spiritually.

♥ In which area(s) do you need restoration or healing? Talk to God in prayer about your need(s).

Day 5
Scripture: Ephesians 1:15-21
15 "For this reason, ever since I heard about your faith in the Lord Jesus and your love for all the saints, 16 I have not stopped giving thanks for you, remembering you in my prayers. 17 I keep asking that the God of our Lord Jesus Christ, the glorious Father, may give you the Spirit of wisdom and revelation, so that you may know Him better. 18 I pray also that the eyes of your heart may be enlightened in order that you may know the hope to which He has called you, the riches of His glorious inheritance in the saints, 19 and His incomparably great power for us who believe. That power is like the working of His mighty strength, 20 which He exerted in Christ when He raised him from the dead and seated Him at His right hand in the heavenly realms, 21 far above all rule and authority, power and dominion, and every title that can be given, not only in the present age but also in the one to come."

* In this passage, Paul is praying for the Ephesians. The sentence is complicated but as you unravel it, note that the first thing Paul requests (verse 17) is that God would give the Ephesian believers wisdom ("insight into the true nature of things") and revelation ("unveiling of God Himself").

* Why does Paul want them to have wisdom and revelation?

♥ Take time right now and pray that God would give you insight and deeper understanding into who He is.

⊶ From Ephesians 1:18b-21 list the three things that Paul prays you may know.

* Think about God's power. What did His power do for Christ?

* Are there any limits on God's power?

* Over the past five days, you have read verses that highlight God's ability to impact people's lives. Record any new insights or revelations you have had.

PAM

God used my abortion to show me–by experience–His mercy and His forgiveness. Praise His Name!

I had shared with my parents that I was going to have an abortion. I think I was probably apprehensive about the actual medical procedure. My previous experience at the gynecologist's office was very painful–when I had gotten an IUD I experienced intense and debilitating cramps. And now I had gotten pregnant with the IUD in place. So, I'm sure I was dreading the abortion even though I was determined to go through with it. At the same time in my life, God had awakened an interest in Him so I was praying about making it through the procedure. And my mother said she would pray for me. It was quite astounding! I was not a believer, yet I sensed God's presence and watch care even as I was having the abortion. I had a certain peace and comfort through the whole procedure. Afterward, the nurse said I would probably bleed and perhaps have cramps; I had neither. She commented on that fact and I glibly said, "That's the power of prayer!"

Whenever I looked back on that incident I would be confused. How could God have been there when what I was doing was sinful? Why did He make the abortion experience so easy for me when it was wrong? How preposterous of me to think that God had answered prayer when I asked that the abortion go well!! I just couldn't understand how to interpret my experience. I didn't share it much because it seemed heretical! He had been there and had protected and comforted me even as I was rebelling and sinning against Him. Several years later when I was doing a Bible study to continue healing from my abortion, I read James 2:13b and it nearly jumped off the page. "Mercy triumphs over judgment." That was it! God definitely has both aspects to His character. He is loving and merciful and He hates sin and will punish it. I would define mercy as having compassion on someone in need and acting to meet the need. And of course, judgment refers to the fact that God is holy and will punish sin. Yet the mercy is greater than the judgment. May I always bless His name! Mercy and judgment met on the cross. His mercy put Christ on the cross and He took the punishment for my sin. How wonderful that His mercy dominates over His judgment! The same is true for you because God's character has not and does not change!

Immediately after I had the abortion, my father picked me up and I spent the weekend with my parents. When I arrived at their home in the afternoon, I went directly to my old bed. My whole body shuddered in revulsion for what I had done. I knew without a shadow of a doubt that abortion was wrong. I climbed in bed and spent what seemed like hours crying. I was deeply convicted and over-whelmed with grief and guilt. I kept admitting to God over and over that I had sinned and I kept begging Him for forgiveness. As I was crying out, it also became very clear to me that abortion was not my only sin; I had committed fornication and I asked forgiveness for that also. I guess that afternoon I saw clearly how disobeying God's directives for living life really brings horrible results. And, thanks to His abundant grace, I experienced God's forgiveness. I don't know how to explain it, but I knew His comfort and I had complete assurance that He had heard me and I was forgiven. To this day, I am confident of His pardon. What a gift!

It wasn't until a year and a half later that I accepted Christ as my personal Saviour and Lord. I had always thought of myself as a nice person and I did good things so I figured I was acceptable to God. But God used my abortion to convince me that I was a sinner. The ugly reality was that I took the life of my child rather than face the public humiliation of being an unwed mother! I couldn't escape the reality that I was out of sync with God and as time passed, I had a growing desire to be right with Him. That lead eventually, to the revelation that Christ was hanging on the cross for my sins, abortion and everything else! I marvel at the way He can take sin and use it for good as it says in *Romans 8:28, "All things work together for good..."* He used my abortion to bring me to Himself.

As I have talked to other women I realize how unusual my experience was. Most women do not experience any healing or forgiveness immediately after having an abortion. God works in different ways with each of us. God's timing is unique for you. However, I am completely sure that He offers deep assurance of forgiveness to anyone who will wrestle with Him and not let go until He grants it. Maybe it will mean even begging God to help you accept forgiveness. I exhort you, to seek with all your heart that assurance from Him–HE can lift the most tremendous burden you have been carrying. Our God is an awesome God and mercy triumphs over judgment!

Chapter Two:
GOD IS WILLING TO HEAL

Hopefully you are now strengthened in your conviction that God is indeed the Almighty Sovereign God over every person, event and situation. He has all power and authority to accomplish what He wills; He can heal you completely. But does He want to exert His power on your behalf? God's ability and power cannot be disconnected from His goodness and His love for you as one of His children. As you read the Scriptures in this chapter, focus on how God expresses His power and might. These attributes are combined with His great mercy and love; the truth is that He is willing to minister to you personally.

Day 1
Scripture: Jeremiah 29:11-13

"For I know the plans I have for you," declares the LORD, "plans to prosper you and not to harm you, plans to give you hope and a future. Then you will call upon me and come and pray to me and I will listen to you."

* What kind of plans or thoughts does God have for you?

♥ Is the reality of Jeremiah 29:11-13 difficult for you to accept? If so, why?

* What response is God looking for on your part?

Scripture: Ephesians 1:4

"For He chose us in Him before the creation of the world to be holy and blameless in His sight. In love He predestined us to be adopted as His sons through Jesus Christ, in accordance with His pleasure and will–."

* Who chose you to be in Christ?

* What was the reason for your adoption?

☙ What does it mean to be holy and blameless?

Do you realize that the deepest, most significant problem in your life was sin? And according to these verses in Ephesians God took care of your deepest need. He chose you to receive forgiveness and redemption in Christ! He reconciled you to Himself through Christ's work on the cross. Accept this truth as evidence of His willingness to heal you and rejoice if you are a believer that He has, in a sense, already "healed" you spiritually.

Day 2
Scripture: Matthew 7:7-11
   "Ask and it will be given to you; seek and you will find; knock and the door will be opened to you. For everyone who asks receives; he who seeks finds; and to him who knocks, the door will be opened. Which of you, if his son asks for bread, will give him a stone? Or if he asks for a fish, will give him a snake? If you, then, though you are evil, know how to give good gifts to your children, how much more will your Father in heaven give good gifts to those who ask Him!"

⚎ What is the promise in these verses?

♥ Identify what it is you need to ask for and take time right now to ask, seek and knock on your heavenly Father's door.

* Read the verses again and meditate on them. Do they imply that God would be willing to give you healing and comfort?

* What good gifts has the Father in heaven already given you?

Day 3
Scripture: Romans 8:28-34
   28*"And we know that in all things God works for the good of those who love Him, who have been called according to his purpose. 29 For those God foreknew He also predestined to be conformed to the likeness of his Son, that He might be the firstborn among many brothers. 30 And those He predestined, He also called; those He called, He also justified; those He justified, He also glorified. 31 What, then, shall we say in response to this? If God is for us, who can be against us? 32 He who did not spare His own Son, but gave Him up for us all–how will He not also, along with Him, graciously give us all things? 33 Who will bring any charge against those whom God has chosen? It is God who justifies. 34 Who is he that condemns? Christ Jesus, who died–more than that, who was raised to life–is at the right hand of God and is also interceding for us."*

↦ List all the verbs of what God has already done for you (Rom 8:28-34).

* What's the promise in verse 28?

* How do you know the promise applies to you?

* From verse 32, how are you assured that God is for you?

* Can anyone bring a charge against you upon which Christ has not already pronounced a verdict of "not guilty'?

♥ Are you harboring any charges against yourself that you need to bring to Jesus and receive His assurance of "not guilty"?

* Verse 34 says that Christ is interceding for you. Look up *intercede* in the dictionary and write the definition here.

Christ is interceding for you! Whatever emotions are welling up, whatever self-condemnation or doubts are surfacing, whatever turmoil–think about Jesus. He is steadily and lovingly talking to the Father on your behalf. Isn't that a wonderful comfort!

Day 4
Scripture: Romans 8:35-39
"Who shall separate us from the love of Christ? Shall trouble or hardship or persecution or famine or nakedness or danger or sword? As it is written: 'For your sake we face death all day long; we are considered as sheep to be slaughtered.' No, in all these things we are more than conquerors through Him who loved us. For I am convinced that neither death nor life, neither angels nor demons, neither the present nor the future, nor any powers, neither height nor depth, nor anything else in all creation, will be able to separate us from the love of God that is in Christ Jesus our Lord."

* From Romans 8:35-39, list the seventeen things which cannot separate us from the love of Christ.

♥ According to this passage, has your abortion(s) separated you from God's love and concern for you personally?

If you have got it in your mind that your abortion has put you in disfavor with God so that He doesn't want to work in your life–you are wrong! Your feelings of condemnation and guilt may be very strong; however, Romans 8 clearly teaches that there is no thing, absolutely nothing, which can separate you from the love of Christ. His love means that He desires and will work toward what is best for you.

Scripture: Mark 9:20-24

"So they brought him. When the spirit saw Jesus, it immediately threw the boy into a convulsion. He fell to the ground and rolled around, foaming at the mouth. Jesus asked the boy's father, 'How long has he been like this?' 'From childhood,' he answered. 'It has often thrown him into fire or water to kill him. But if you can do anything, take pity on us and help us.' 'If you can?' said Jesus. 'Everything is possible for him who believes.' Immediately the boy's father exclaimed, 'I do believe; help me overcome my unbelief!' "

* How many years had the boy been demon-possessed?

* What was the father's request?

⊷ What does Jesus say is possible for the person who believes?

* Although your abortion(s) may have happened years ago, does the time element affect Jesus' ability or willingness to heal?

In the passage, the issue wasn't whether Jesus had the ability and willingness to heal, but whether the father had faith to believe Jesus. If you are having trouble believing that God is willing and able to heal you, pray and ask God to help you overcome your unbelief.

Day 5

Scripture: Philippians 2:12-13

"Therefore, my dear friends, as you have always obeyed–not only in my presence, but now much more in my absence–continue to work out your salvation with fear and trembling, for it is God who works in you to will and to act according to His good purpose."

These verses almost sound like a contradiction. On one hand, you are instructed to "work out your salvation with fear and trembling" and on the other hand you are told that "it is God who works in you to will and to act for His good purpose." Working out your salvation is the idea of showing in everyday life what God has done in saving you. You are a new creature and have responsibility to grow in godly living. This work on your part is done with fear and trembling, meaning with awe and reverence toward God. Ultimately, though, it is God who gives you the will (desire) and ability to obey Him. Both divine enablement and human responsibility are involved in your spiritual growth.

* Write out your understanding of Philippians 2:12-13, including how it applies to your abortion(s).

☙ In order to heal, what are your responsibilities and what are God's?

Scripture: Philippians 1:4-6

"In all my prayers for all of you, I always pray with joy because of your partnership in the gospel from the first day until now, being confident of this, that he who began a good work in you will carry it on to completion until the day of Christ Jesus."

* What's the good work that God has begun in you?

*What does this promise about your spiritual growth?

Rejoice! God is at work in you. He does desire to heal you and to further conform you to the image of His Son and your Lord, Jesus Christ.

I trust the Scriptures and your meditations during the past two chapters have convinced you (at least intellectually) that God is able and God is willing to heal you emotionally and spiritually and to restore you totally. Is this your desire?

♥ Confront yourself with the bottom line question—do you believe God or don't you? Will you entrust yourself to Him and open up to Him or won't you? It's similar to the question Jesus asked the man in John 5:6 when He said, *"Do you want to get well?"*

* Right now take time to pray earnestly and honestly before God. Tell Him what is on your heart. What are your fears? Ask Him to calm your anxieties. What are your doubts about trusting Him? Ask Him to build your faith. Thank Him for His ability and willingness to heal you.

PEGGY

During the course of my abortion recovery counseling (I was in a 10 step Bible study program, my second attempt at seeking healing after a lapse of many years since my four abortions), I sensed that I was again, merely going through the motions/ exercises of this healing program, but not really benefiting. I was in deception with regard to God's true character/nature...and had been all of my life. But I did not know this. My thought was that God was going to punish me for the remainder of my days on this earth. I just accepted that. I was a murderer, not able to be forgiven, with no redeeming value.

I came home one day from the day's counseling session, greatly fatigued to the core of my being and giving in to depression (I was in denial with regard to all of the aspects/fallout from my four abortions, and even when alone I had never given in to the reality of what I was feeling). But this day was different somehow. It was a bright and sunny afternoon but I put on my pajamas and crawled in to bed; something I had never done before, and I just wept, a very long time, with abandon. I was furious with myself and I was far from Father God. I thought of Him as merely the hovering hand of justice waiting to pass sentence on me and my miserable existence. The combination of my self-loathing and selfishness seemed to be suffocating me. How I despised myself, and thought I would never be in any other place in my mind. My usual remedy to this was to "buck up" and go to that place of denial in my mind and step out as the person I wanted everyone to see, and to cover my real self. I was too horrible to be experienced!

But this day I was unable to do that, even. I was breaking somehow. And it frightened me. So I called out to God...through my tears, and closed my eyes at an attempt to rest my weary self. I do not know if I slept; but I know that God blessed me with His beloved grace and mercy in a way that astounded me–through what I can only describe as a vision, perhaps a dream, or even waking thoughtfulness, I do not know. But here is what I experienced:

I saw an extraordinarily large lap, a seated personage, covered in folds of lovely and soft white cloth of some sort, there was no flesh visible, no features other than this huge robe clad lap. And I was placed upon that lap, and great arms covered in folds of that same material enfolded me there, on that lap, and held me there. My sensation recall is not of the feeling of touch, but rather what came over me was the most incredulous sense of safe keeping and the love of Father God...I almost could not take it in; it overwhelmed me. I cried and cried, but not from pain, as I had been doing earlier, but rather from a sense of, "How can this all be for me...how can You possibly love me?"

Yet with absolute certainty and with clarity I knew that God was loving me; that He always had, and that I was in the throes of the very first time of receiving that love, that mercy, that grace, that forgiveness...and gently, so very gently, did His Holy Spirit reveal to me that I had been in deception about God's character, thinking of Him only in terms of an authoritative and merciless judge and that the only sentence that could be passed on me would be condemnation. I was living under that condemnation, which was from Satan, the father of lies, and I was believing that God was a God of condemnation only. My sin had separated me from Him, yes, but the deception from the enemy kept me from experiencing God's love. I would not allow myself to experience love...I thought I was unworthy in God's eyes.

But then I remembered at that moment, JESUS, and the Truth of the matter at hand...the piercing power of the Word of God was doing its work in me and I knew for absolute certain that Jesus was sent to shed His blood for the blood that I had shed, that of my own children, and that my sin was covered, died for, risen for and FORGIVEN, once and for all. Paid in full. I did not have to keep on paying and paying and paying; I could not make up for my sinful choices.

In that vision I truly experienced the love of our Father God and I cannot recall that time without shedding tears of wonder and joy and a heart full of praise and thanksgiving that the victory over my sin is a reality! And God's grace, unfathomable as it is to me, is sufficient for me, even unto death.

Chapter Three:
THE SITUATION

For many women, the abortion goes underground. It is such a devastating experience and so traumatic that denial takes over to shield you from pain. So for many of you it may have been years since you consciously thought through the whole situation. I'm going to ask you to re-experience it by answering a few questions. I recognize that these next five days will be difficult emotionally; yet they are crucial.

Take time now and throughout the process to pray and ask God to search your heart and to bring the truth to the light. Try not to censure your thoughts and feelings as they resurface and you write them down. Also, ask God to come near and comfort you when this process becomes difficult. If there isn't enough space provided, feel free to add your own pages. Take your time and get your memories down on paper. If you have had more than one abortion, I would suggest that you answer these questions for each one.

Note to group: When you meet as a group to discuss this chapter, divide your time equally between members and give each woman time to share her story. If someone is not comfortable in sharing, then go on to the next participant; no pressure here!

Day 1
* How did you get pregnant? Write out all the circumstances surrounding your pregnancy including your relationship with the father. What was it like to find out that you were pregnant?

Day 2

* What were all the external and internal voices or forces that led to your decision to abort? External forces could include the world's value system, advice from an abortion clinic, your parents, the father of the child, friends, etc. Internal pressures would be your own fears and desires. What were all the reasons you had for choosing abortion?

Day 3

* What were your feelings and thoughts before, during and after the actual abortion? Try to reconstruct the actual experience and describe what it was like for you.

Day 4

* During the whole process of getting pregnant, making the decision to abort, and experiencing an abortion, what did you think about God? Describe the part God played in your thought and/or experience.

Day 5
* Think of all the people who were involved in your abortion. List them (father of baby, parents, friends, doctor, nurses, etc.) Identify the feelings or attitudes you have now for each one.

Allow me to pray for you and with you.

"Dear Lord God, thank you for helping each woman bring her abortion and her responses to the light. I praise You that You gave comfort and held each one close in Your everlasting arms during this process. Now, strengthen each woman by Your Spirit; increase our faith and root and ground us in Your love. Fill my sisters with all the fullness of God as they continue on. Bless You, Lord! Amen."

SUSAN

I believe that all things work together for good for those who love God and are called according to His purpose. But there are still many times in life when accepting that is extremely difficult. Particularly when for a long period of time we live with the horrible guilt of the evil we have done.

For 20 years after I had an abortion, I, for the most part, completely closed and barricaded my thoughts regarding that horrible incident. It was so unlike me to commit a sin that grotesque. I had always been able to behave so well that people admired me for my Christian testimony, my upstanding behavior and my godly wisdom. No one could ever know what I had done, for I was nearly perfect in my own righteousness. As a child, I was taught about God and the Bible. I never doubted that God existed and that the Bible was true. I knew that Jesus had died for the sins of mankind and I believed that. I knew that I was a sinner and yet I never believed it. I had been taught the law. I knew what was right and what was wrong and I tried my utmost to not do anything wrong. I wanted to be right and perfect and loved.

I knew it was wrong for me to choose to date non-Christians. But as soon as I went to college and was away from my family and friends and since no Christian boys asked me out, I felt it wouldn't hurt to "just date" non-Christian boys. After all, I wasn't going to marry one.

Playing with fire is a dangerous business, however; and it wasn't long before I got burned. I became sexually active and all the while, hid it from most of the people who cared about me, not wanting anyone to know that I wasn't the perfect Christian girl. I ended up deceiving myself the most and when I became pregnant, the option of not having an abortion was never more than a fleeting thought. My reputation was at stake and I was not about to have it soiled. I didn't think of this problem as a baby or an actual life. It was merely a missed period. To further affirm my decision to have an abortion, the very kind doctor who performed it assured me that this was no big deal. I wasn't very far along, he explained, and no big instruments were necessary. Just a little vacuum cleaner and a pinch of pain. He was right. But with the pinch of pain came the realization that comes to every killer after the life is taken. An overwhelming feeling of guilt, an instant sense of undoing, the terrible knowledge that what is done, is done, and can never be changed. I cried and prayed for forgiveness for the next 48 hours.

A person cannot come to terms with such wrong without thinking it through and realizing their heart. So the years that were spent with my mind's door shut concerning this incident rapidly grew into a separation between God and me, and the peace in my heart that I had at one time enjoyed became a distant memory. I tried everything I could think of to get the feeling back. God was gracious to me. Eventually I married and our first son was born. I believed that God had answered my prayers for forgiveness. Six more children were born and I marveled each time at God's graciousness to me. I never in all those years practiced a consistent birth control. I was going to give birth to as many lives as I could in the hope of canceling out the murder of one. Still, things weren't right. I would tell myself, "God has forgiven you, it's you that can't forgive yourself." Soon that almost sounded like a holy idea, so I clung to it. I would continue to work at my redemption.

It seems that one thing doesn't have anything to do with another and yet God does that working together thing of His. As the years progressed, it became apparent to me that the man I had chosen for my husband, was not the man I thought he was. After 22 years of marriage, he betrayed me. In the sleepless nights after that discovery, I came to a startling realization about myself. My husband may have betrayed me, but I had callously and calculatingly taken the life of my child. I was a sinner. My husband wasn't a worse sinner than me; nor were killers on death row worse sinners than me; I, like Paul, was chief among sinners. My attempts to work for salvation were hopeless failures. My self-righteousness was nothing more than filthy rags. I needed God! His deliverance was what I longed for and it was available through Jesus Christ.

Sin comes naturally. It is easily covered and masked and we learn to live with it. Only when our spirits are undone, when we actually see our sinful hearts, then we become the putty and the clay from which God is able to work all things together for His good.

Chapter Four:
SUBMIT TO GOD

In the first two weeks, you looked at God's ability and willingness to heal you re: your abortion experience(s). Last week you were asked to revisit the abortion(s) and reflect upon several aspects of your response to your pregnancy(ies). No doubt the recollection of that time has stirred up memories mixed with many emotions. At this point in the study, we are going to shift gears and work through those emotions and responses by applying the biblical commands found in James 4:7-10.

Scripture: James 4:7-10

"Submit yourselves, then, to God. Resist the devil, and he will flee from you. Come near to God and He will come near to you. Wash your hands, you sinners, and purify your hearts, you double-minded. Grieve, mourn and wail. Change your laughter to mourning and your joy to gloom. Humble yourselves before the Lord, and He will lift you up."

* List the seven commands.

The first command is to submit yourselves to God. Submit is a Greek military term meaning "to rank under" or "to obey." It includes the idea of surrendering or yielding to another's authority. It may seem odd to include submission as a part of your healing, but I believe it is important for you to yield your abortion experience(s) to God. Do you see Him as your authority? Are you willing to do whatever He might ask of you? Will you choose to submit? The goal of this chapter is for you to understand various aspects of submission to God and then for you to willingly yield to God's authority with regard to your abortion(s).

Day 1
Scripture: Isaiah 45:5,9, & 12

5 "I am the LORD, and there is no other; apart from me there is no God. I will strengthen you, though you have not acknowledged me,..."

9 "Woe to him who quarrels with his Maker, to him who is but a potsherd among the potsherds on the ground. Does the clay say to the potter, 'What are you making?' Does your work say, 'He has no hands'?"

12 "It is I who made the earth and created mankind upon it. My own hands stretched out the heavens; I marshaled their starry hosts."

↔ What reasons to submit to God are found in the previous verses?

Scripture Isaiah 64:8

"Yet, O LORD, you are our Father. We are the clay, you are the potter; we are all the work of your hand."

* In this verse, you are being compared with clay. What are the characteristics of clay?

* How does the idea that you are clay help you understand submission to God?

❤ What are your struggles with being the clay?

Day 2

Scripture: Romans 12:1

"Therefore, I urge you, brothers, in view of God's mercy, to offer your bodies as living sacrifices, holy and pleasing to God–which is your spiritual worship."

* What are you commanded to offer or yield to God?

↔ What does it mean to be a living sacrifice?

Scripture: Romans 6:13

"Do not offer the parts of your body to sin, as instruments of wickedness, but rather offer yourselves to God, as those who have been brought from death to life; and offer the parts of your body to Him as instruments of righteousness."

* What do you think is meant by "parts of your body"?

* This verse implies that you have a choice. To what can you yield the parts of your body?

Scripture: II Corinthians 10:4-5
"The weapons we fight with are not the weapons of the world. On the contrary, they have divine power to demolish strongholds. We demolish arguments and every pretension that sets itself up against the knowledge of God, and we take captive every thought to make it obedient to Christ."

* Note the phrase "we take captive every thought to make it obedient to Christ." What does this mean in your life?

* Review today's three Scriptures. What are you commanded to submit or yield to God?

❤ Is there any part of your life that has not been submitted to His authority?

Day 3
Scripture: James 4:7a
"Submit yourselves, then, to God."

* To whom are you called to submit?

Scripture: Lamentations 3:22-25
"Because of the Lord's great love we are not consumed, for His compassions never fail. They are new every morning; great is your faithfulness. I say to myself, 'The LORD is my portion; therefore I will wait for Him.' The LORD is good to those whose hope is in Him, to the one who seeks Him."

➼ Stop and meditate on these verses. Who is this God to whom you are called to submit and what is He like?

* Does this biblical description of God line up with your view of God?

Scripture: Hebrews 12:7-11

"Endure hardship as discipline; God is treating you as sons. For what son is not disciplined by his father? If you are not disciplined (and everyone undergoes discipline), then you are illegitimate children and not true sons. Moreover, we have all had human fathers who disciplined us and we respected them for it. How much more should we submit to the Father of our spirits and live! Our fathers disciplined us for a little while as they thought best; but God disciplines us for our good, that we may share in His holiness. No discipline seems pleasant at the time, but painful. Later on, however, it produces a harvest of righteousness and peace for those who have been trained by it."

This passage encourages us to submit to the Father (verse 9) in terms of His discipline. Discipline refers to training or instruction, and not to punishment. I believe this passage is a call to see hardship and suffering as God-ordained, designed for His good purpose.

* According to these verses, what's the purpose of God's discipline?

* How is God's discipline consistent with His nature?

If you have fears about letting go and letting God control your life, remember who God is and what He is like. He is loving and unchanging. He is completely unselfish. He is good. Everything He orchestrates in your life is for your ultimate good. Even His discipline which seems painful is a good thing and intended to bring good fruits in your life.

♥ Recount an incident in which God showed you His goodness, love and faithfulness.

Day 4

*What does submission to God look like? The answer to that question can be gleaned from observing Jesus who is our model of submission. Read the following verses and write down all your observations about how and what Christ submitted to the Father.

Scripture: John 5:19

    "Jesus gave them this answer: 'I tell you the truth, the Son can do nothing by Himself; He can do only what He sees His Father doing, because whatever the Father does the Son also does…' "

Scripture: John 5:30

    "By myself I can do nothing; I judge only as I hear, and my judgment is just, for I seek not to please myself but Him who sent me."

Scripture: John 6:38

    "For I have come down from heaven not to do my will but to do the will of Him who sent me."

Scripture: John 7:16-17

    "Jesus answered, 'My teaching is not my own. It comes from Him who sent me. If any one chooses to do God's will, he will find out whether my teaching comes from God or whether I speak on my own…' "

Scripture: John 8:28-29

    "So Jesus said, 'When you have lifted up the Son of Man, then you will know who I am and that I do nothing on my own but speak just what the Father has taught me. The one who sent me is with me; He has not left me alone, for I always do what pleases Him.' "

Scripture: Luke 22:42

    "Father, if you are willing, take this cup from me; yet not my will, but yours be done."

✏ Summarize all your observations about what submission looked like in Jesus' life.

❤ How can you implement Christ-like submission in your life? Is this easy for you?

Day 5

What does submission look like in your life, particularly in relation to your abortion(s)? I want to make three points regarding submission:

1) <u>Submission involves a belief that God is God.</u>

Scripture: Isaiah 45:21b-22

"And there is no God apart from me, a righteous God and a Savior; there is none but me. Turn to me and be saved, all you ends of the earth, for I am God, and there is no other."

* Do you believe that God is God?

* Do you believe that God is the ultimate authority of the universe?

* Do you believe that God is <u>your</u> authority?

2) <u>Submission involves making a choice.</u>

It is a command and yet you can choose whether or not you submit. God does not force us to obey; we are not puppets. You may have difficulty placing yourself under God's authority and His control because of trust issues. The human desire for control and independence (We are rebels at heart!) must be denied by meditating on the character of God. He does know best and He does want the best for you.

* Will you, in faith, put yourself under His authority?

* Will you allow Him, through His Word, to "dictate" how you should live?

3) <u>Submission involves active obedience.</u>

Scripture: Matthew 21:28-31a (Jesus tells a parable)

28 "What do you think? There was a man who had two sons. He went to the first and said, 'Son, go and work today in the vineyard.' 29 'I will not,' he answered, but later he changed his mind and went. 30 Then the father went to the other son and said the same thing. He answered, 'I will, sir,' but he did not go. 31 Which of the two did what his father wanted?" "The first, they answered."

* In this parable, what did submission to the Father involve?

❧ How do the three underlined points listed previously affect your willingness to yield your abortion(s) to God?

In the following pages, through His Word, God may ask you to: think differently, to repent, to receive and extend forgiveness, or to accept His deep love for you. I want to encourage you to purpose in your heart to submit to His authority and tender working in you. Remember His plans for you are for good!

♥ Is there anything that God is asking you to yield to Him right now?

JULIE

As a senior in high school I thought I had met the man with whom I wanted to spend the rest of my life. After a few months of dating we started having sex. I thought having sex meant we were committed to each other. I was always afraid of becoming pregnant. Even though I was with the man I was hoping to one day marry, I wasn't ready for the responsibility of raising a child. I was also ashamed at the thought of other people knowing that I was having sex. When I did become pregnant during my second year in college, the horrifying reality of my boyfriend's response caused a shift in my fairy tale. He said that I would need to get an abortion.

I believed that he would leave me if I didn't get an abortion. I thought he would not be attracted to me during my pregnancy. I began to have destructive thoughts toward the pregnancy. Before, I had hated abortion and I judged the women who had them. Now, I was joining these women of whom I disapproved. I was betraying the core of my own moral structure. All that I cared about was keeping this relationship. My selfishness led me to believe that I was doing the right thing by having an abortion because I wouldn't be able to take good care of the child under my present circumstances.

One day we will start a family when things are ready I would tell myself. I hoped that I wouldn't be punished for having this abortion. I hoped I wouldn't one day have a deformed baby. I started using drugs to help with my fears. I started making decisions that led me down pathways away from hope. Finally, after about seven or so years, the relationship ripped apart. Geographically, I moved far away and he moved even further.

In my attempt to replace this guy with someone just like him, I began a relationship with a man who carried a Bible with him from time to time. One day I picked up his Bible and began reading in the New Testament. I knew in the deepest darkness of my heart that the words I had read were true. I kept saying over and over in my mind "I believe this." I began weeping and from that day on I have believed that Jesus Christ is who He says He is. This was the beginning of my relationship with the One True Love who is my LORD Jesus Christ.

I moved back to the area where I was born. And I got involved in a ministry that included abortion recovery as part of its mission. As a volunteer I was required to participate in a program for my own healing. It had been sixteen years since my abortion. I was starving for forgiveness. I was still blind to what I had actually done. I had no idea that my baby had a form, a beating heart, hands, feet, eyes, a little belly. I had believed that IT was just a clot of blood and that nothing had been formed yet. The reality of my abortion was finally being able to surface. Fortunately, I was able to walk through the wounded place with another woman who had chosen abortion. As we walked, the LORD brought the circumstances, Scripture readings and other people into our lives that demonstrated His great power of forgiveness, His love and His faithfulness.

Psalm 32:1-5 is where God showed me how to cry.

"Blessed is he whose transgression is forgiven,
Whose sin is covered.
Blessed is the man to whom the LORD does not impute iniquity,
And in whose spirit there is no deceit.

When I kept silent, my bones grew old
through my groaning all the day long.
For day and night Your hand was heavy upon me.

My vitality was turned into the drought of summer. Selah
I acknowledged my sin to You,
And my iniquity I have not hidden.
I said, 'I will confess my transgressions to the LORD.'
And You forgave the iniquity of my sin." Selah

In preparing for a memorial service for my child, God helped me to experience the significance of not only what I had done, but more importantly, what He had done in order to forgive me. At first, I had a hard time accepting His forgiveness. The guilt and shame that surrounded my abortion prevented me from experiencing His great mercy. It has been through looking to Jesus and His victory over death on the cross that I have been able to let go of my grip on the sin and allow Him to take it. Faced with the verses in Psalm 32, I began to understand the significance of not only God's love but also His forgiveness. I acknowledged my sin to God and accepted His forgiveness.

In Psalm 30:11-12 it reads, *"You have turned for me my mourning into dancing, You have put off my sackcloth and clothed me with gladness, To the end that my glory may sing praise to You and not be silent. O LORD my God, I will give thanks to You forever."*

Jesus Christ is our High Priest. He is our King! He is the One who heals. In Him we have forgiveness. Through Him we have deliverance. Worthy is the Lamb of God to receive glory, honor and praise.

Chapter Five:
RESIST THE DEVIL

The second half of James 4:7 contains a second instruction, "Resist the devil, and he will flee from you." What does this statement mean? Primarily, it describes a defensive stance against an opponent. An analogy might be if someone comes at you with a weapon intending to harm you. Instead of either running away or fighting, you are to stand and oppose this person. And this verse promises that your enemy will actually run from you!

The person you are to stand and oppose is the devil or Satan. As Satan's name, "Accuser," suggests, he is a liar and a destroyer. He opposes God; Satan's goal is to undermine God's authority and working in our lives. He brings temptations to sin: to disobey God, to pursue our own way instead of submitting to God's authority. He plants thoughts of condemnation, doubt, and fear in our minds.

So, how do you obey the command to resist Satan? Most likely, Satan is not going to come in person, so the verse is not talking about resisting in a physical sense. Instead, I think it refers to opposing Satan's schemes in your mind. When wrong thoughts and desires come your way, you are to resist and not give in. Stand firm. The key to having a strong defense is to know and believe the Bible.

As your accuser and destroyer, Satan would have you believe lies about abortion that cause you to doubt God's mercy and forgiveness for you. The goal of this chapter is to replace your wrong beliefs with the truth of Scripture–to learn to resist the devil in your thoughts. Meditate on these verses and let God speak to you personally through His Word.

Day 1
Wrong belief: The aborted fetus wasn't a real person.

Scripture: Psalm 139:13-16
"For you created my inmost being; you knit me together in my mother's womb. I praise you because I am fearfully and wonderfully made; your works are wonderful, I know that full well. My frame was not hidden from you when I was made in the secret place. When I was woven together in the depths of the earth, your eyes saw my unformed body. All the days ordained for me were written in your book before one of them came to be."

* To whom is the psalmist speaking when he says, "For you created my inmost being"?

* When did God know about the existence of the psalmist?

Scripture: Job 10:8-12

"*Your hands shaped me and made me. Will you now turn and destroy me? Remember that you molded me like clay. Will you now turn me to dust again? Did you not pour me out like milk and curdle me like cheese, clothe me with skin and flesh and knit me together with bones and sinews? You gave me life and showed me kindness, and in your providence watched over my spirit.*"

➼ According to Psalm 139 and Job 10, where does life come from, and when does it begin?

Scripture: Judges 13:2-5,24

"*A certain man of Zorah, named Manoah, from the clan of the Danites, had a wife who was sterile and remained childless. The angel of the Lord appeared to her and said, 'You are sterile and childless, but you are going to conceive and have a son. Now see to it that you drink no wine or other fermented drink and that you do not eat anything unclean, because you will conceive and give birth to a son. No razor may be used on his head, because the boy is to be a Nazarite, set apart to God from birth, and he will begin the deliverance of Israel from the hands of the Philistines.'*"

24 "*The woman gave birth to a boy and named him Samson. He grew and the Lord blessed him...*"

* Who knew about Manoah's wife's conception before she did?

* What was predicted about the child's character even in the womb?

In each of these Scriptures God knew everything about each individual even before conception. Furthermore, God is identified as the creator of life. This may be a difficult truth to accept. However, remember that it is the truth that will set you free!

❤ What did you believe about life when you had your abortion(s) and what do you believe now?

Day 2
Wrong belief: Abortion is not a sin.

Abortion is legal and many people see nothing wrong with it. Perhaps you and others you know believe that abortion is a woman's choice and that it's not a moral issue. But how does God look at it?

Scripture: Exodus 21:22-25
"If men who are fighting hit a pregnant woman and she gives birth prematurely but there is no serious injury, the offender must be fined whatever the woman's husband demands and the court allows. But if there is serious injury, you are to take life for life, eye for eye, tooth for tooth, hand for hand, foot for foot, burn for burn, wound for wound, bruise for bruise."

* What was the consequence if a pregnant woman or her child was injured?

* What does the severity of the Old Testament law tell you about the value God places on a human's life?

Scripture: Proverbs 6:16-17
"There are six things the Lord hates, seven that are detestable to Him: haughty eyes, a lying tongue, hands that shed innocent blood, a heart that devises wicked schemes, feet that are quick to rush into evil, a false witness who pours out lies and a man who stirs up dissension among brothers."

* List the seven things God hates.

* Which one would apply to abortion?

🖙 In God's eyes, is abortion a sin? According to the passage above, how does He feel about it?

At this point you may be tempted to go to a place of condemnation and guilt. It is true that your abortion(s) was sin; it is true that God hates sin and will punish it. However, it is also true that mercy triumphs over judgment! Listen carefully to God's words to you:

Scripture: Romans 5:9

    "Since we have now been justified by His blood, how much more shall we be saved from God's wrath through Him!"

Scripture: Romans 8:1

    "There is therefore now no condemnation to those who are in Christ Jesus, who do not walk according to the flesh, but according to the Spirit."

❤ Explain how Christ's blood, which He shed on the cross for you, affects the punishment for your abortion(s).

    As C.J. Mahaney writes, "Don't buy the lie that cultivating condemnation and wallowing in your shame is somehow pleasing to God, or that a constant low grade guilt will somehow promote holiness and spiritual maturity. It's just the opposite. God is glorified when we believe with all our hearts that those who trust in Christ can never be condemned."

Day 3

Wrong belief: It wasn't my choice to abort; I was a victim of the situation. My parents, boyfriend, husband, relatives or friends made me abort, so I am not personally responsible.

Scripture: Read Genesis 2:15-17; Gen 3:6

    15 "The Lord God took the man and put him in the Garden of Eden to work it and take care of it. 16 And the Lord God commanded the man, 'You are free to eat from any tree in the garden; 17 but you must not eat from the tree of the knowledge of good and evil, for when you eat of it you will surely die.' "

    6 "When the woman saw that the fruit of the tree was good for food and pleasing to the eye, and also desirable for gaining wisdom, she took some and ate it. She also gave some to her husband, who was with her, and he ate it."

* Who sinned? Eve? Adam? or both of them?

* What was the sin?

Scripture: Genesis 3:11-13

    11 "And He (God) said, 'Who told you that you were naked? Have you eaten from the tree that I commanded you not to eat from?' 12 The man said, 'The woman you put here with me—she gave me some fruit from the tree, and I ate it.' 13 Then the Lord God said to the woman, 'What is this you have done?' The woman said, 'The serpent deceived me, and I ate.' "

‿ Did Adam "own" his sin? Did Eve "own" hers?

* Notice that God addressed each of them separately. What does this indicate about who God held accountable for the sin?

Scripture: Romans 14:12

    "So then, each of us will give an account of himself to God."

♥ Though there may have been several influences in your life to abort, ultimately who made the decision? Who will God hold accountable?

    Remember the good news! Since you are in Christ, you are now righteous in God's eyes, because on the cross, God held Jesus accountable for your sin (II Corinthians 5:21).

Day 4
Wrong belief: God won't forgive me because what I did is too terrible.

Scripture: Colossians 2:13

    "When you were dead in your sins and in the uncircumcision of your sinful nature, God made you alive with Christ. He forgave us all our sins."

‿ At salvation, what did God do? How many sins did God forgive? (This would be a good time to reflect and make a list of the sins God has forgiven.)

* Does *"all"* in the Colossians verse include abortion?

Scripture: Hebrews 9:14

    "How much more, then, will the blood of Christ, who through the eternal Spirit offered Himself unblemished to God, cleanse our consciences from acts that lead to death, so that we may serve the living God!"

♥ Do you struggle with guilt? Is it real or false guilt?

* According to this verse, what does the blood of Christ do?

* When you are freed from a guilty conscience, what are you free to do?

Scripture: I Timothy 1:15-17
      "Here is a trustworthy saying that deserves full acceptance: Christ Jesus came into the world to save sinners–of whom I am the worst. But for that very reason I was shown mercy so that in me, the worst of sinners, Christ Jesus might display His unlimited patience as an example for those who would believe on Him and receive eternal life. Now to the King eternal, immortal, invisible, the only God, be honor and glory forever and ever. Amen."

* Paul calls himself the worst sinner. Did God forgive him?

* What is Paul's focus—his sin or God's mercy? What is your focus?

* Do you believe that God has forgiven you on the basis of Christ's death on the cross?

Day 5
Wrong belief: God is now or in the future going to punish me. Perhaps you think, "Because I had an abortion(s) I now _____"
                                                                fill in the blank
possibilities: have an unhappy marriage, am single, can't conceive children, don't relate well with the children I have, fear a future punishment."

Scripture: II Samuel 11 & 12 provide the background for the verses you are going to look at. In summary, King David commits adultery with a beautiful woman named Bathsheba while her husband Uriah is at war. She conceives, David orchestrates her husband's death in battle and then takes Bathsheba as his wife. Later, the prophet Nathan confronts David about his sins.

Scripture: II Samuel 12:13-14; 18a

    13 *"Then David said to Nathan, 'I have sinned against the Lord.' Nathan replied, 'The Lord has taken away your sin. You are not going to die. 14 But because by doing this you have made the enemies of the Lord show utter contempt, the son born to you will die.' " 18 "On the seventh day the child died."*

* Was David forgiven for his sin?

* Why did the child die?

Scripture: Galatians 6:7-8

    "Do not be deceived: God cannot be mocked. A man reaps what he sows. The one who sows to please his sinful nature, from that nature will reap destruction; the one who sows to please the Spirit, from the Spirit will reap eternal life."

↢ What's the important biblical principle taught in these verses?

    Nowhere in Scripture do we find God punishing His children! And if you have received Jesus Christ as your Savior, you are one of His children! He is not punishing you! However, He does discipline His children for our good, and He does allow us to reap what we have sown.

    In my case, if I had been married when I conceived, I would not have chosen to abort my child. The sin of fornication, in a sense, led to the sin of abortion. A result of my fornication was abortion, just like an outgrowth of David's adultery was the murder of Uriah. And, of course, then God has consequences for our sin. When God revealed the link between fornication and abortion to me, I made a promise to Him that I would never again have sex outside of marriage. My point in sharing this is to show how experiencing the negative consequences of our sins can be used by God in positive ways.

♥ How might God want to use the consequences (difficult situations) related to your abortion(s) to make you more like Christ?

    It is also very possible that the way you filled in the blank on the previous page has nothing to do with your abortion(s); there is no link except in your mind and interpretation. Ask God to show you the truth about your particular situation. Remember! God does bring good for you out of *all* circumstances.

MAURA

"You will keep him in perfect peace, whose mind is stayed on You, because he trusts in You." Isaiah 26:3 "And let the peace of God rule in your hearts..." Colossians 3:15. God wants us to have peace by guarding our minds and hearts, but I didn't do that 35 years ago.

I was not a typical teenage girl. I was a "goody-goody"; extremely naïve; did not like shopping; I even went to church every week. Yet there was no personal, intimate relationship with the Lord.

"Seek ye first the kingdom of God and all His righteousness..." Matthew 6:33. Even though I was a "good girl" on the outside, I did what I thought best and did not seek God's counsel. Inside I had a growing curiosity and anxiety about hedonistic lifestyles and the popularity those lifestyles seemed to bring. I saw this on television and among my peers and I believed the lies: "All of the popular girls have boyfriends; I need a boyfriend. Something must be wrong with me if I don't have a boyfriend. My clothes aren't cool. I need cool clothes. I need to look like the popular girls." Soon, my attire went from jeans and sweaters and sneakers to more revealing outfits and high heels. Sunbathing in bikinis on the beach became my favorite pastime.

I remember talking to a close friend about a young man I was dating and "crazy" about. He took me to dinner and a movie and we hung out at his house. I felt obligated to do things that I was not comfortable doing, but I was afraid to say no, in fear that he would break up with me. We did not have intercourse but we did everything else. I constantly thought of going further; it was always on my mind. When I told my close friend, her response was, "You can't get pregnant just thinking about it!" Well, that statement couldn't be further from the truth; sin begins in our minds. I continued to resist him and he broke off our relationship and went with a girl who "did." My heart was broken. I thought obsessively, "If only I had done it, we would still be together." Later that year he was killed in a car accident. I was crushed emotionally. I didn't guard my heart and mind but instead chose to become obsessed with sinful thoughts.

Sin was planted and it lead to death just like it says in James 1:15. The few years that followed found me in an abortion clinic three times. I believed the lie the medical professionals told me, "It is only a glob of tissue." Frightened and all alone, I tried to bury every thought and emotion related to this devastating time in my life. This led only to an increase in my debauched lifestyle. For 25 years I tried to suppress all emotion; but the shame, guilt, worry, fear and anger topped with alcohol use destroyed me. I believed more lies, from the "father of lies," the devil, "Oh, don't worry about it, have a drink. Take your mind off your problems; let's go out for a drink." And, "I can't make it on my own. I cannot support myself and my two sons. I can't be without a man in my life."

Then as a divorced mother, cohabitating with another man, I couldn't even go to church. Silent prayers to God and crying myself to sleep kept me functional during the day and finally led me back to church. I had come to the end of myself. God placed this

Scripture verse in my memory and I recited it every waking moment, *"Trust in the Lord with all your heart, and lean not on your own understanding; in all your ways acknowledge Him, and He shall direct your path." Proverbs 3:5-6*

On July 11, 2001, I surrendered my life to Jesus Christ. A few months later, afraid I was doing the wrong thing, I moved out and stopped cohabitating. I can honestly say that since then, my life has been a wonderful journey of living for the Lord, filled with forgiveness, hope, peace and healing. I have been baptized, my two sons accepted the Lord as their Savior and have been baptized, and now I am married to a wonderful Christian husband. I feel blessed to have such an awesome God! Praise God!

Chapter Six:
DRAW NIGH AND MOURN

In this chapter you will study two commands simultaneously. James 4:8a says, "Come near to God and He will come near to you." Verse 9 says, "Grieve, mourn and wail. Change your laughter to mourning and your joy to gloom." The good news is that God is gracious and desires to be close to you and the bad news is that you have sinned against Him. I've decided to combine these two commands because conviction of sin without hope leads to guilt and condemnation and the good news of God's grace without the reality of sin doesn't make sense. The goal of this chapter is twofold: 1) to help you own your sin and to be broken over it and 2) to draw you close to your Redeemer so you experience assurance of His forgiveness.

Day 1
Scripture: James 4:8a
> *"Come near to God, and He will come near to you."*

*What might that look like in your life?

Come near is the idea of approaching someone, of coming into one's presence. Because the blood of Jesus Christ has paid for your sins and has brought peace with God, you can come or approach God with confidence. I think this command refers to coming close to God emotionally and it promises to result in an intimate personal relationship with Him. To make this type of closeness a reality requires time in prayer and the Word, in humility before Him. Remember, the One you are drawing near to loves you beyond your greatest longings!

In James 4:8a, what is God's promise to you?

Scripture: James 4:9
> *"Grieve, mourn and wail. Change your laughter to mourning and your joy to gloom."*

This command is emotionally very difficult. It represents a mandate in how you respond to sin. You are asked to experience how utterly detestable your sin is to God; to feel the weight of your sin and its repugnance to a Holy God. Your emotional responses might include sorrow, weeping and mourning. True repentance is more than an intellectual assent that you have sinned. In repentance your thoughts and emotions are both engaged as you realize how displeasing your sin is to God. I believe that genuine repentance is a work of God's grace in our hearts.

* With regard to our sin, how does regret differ from repentance?

* Pray that over the next two days God will search your heart; He will give grace to allow true repentance; and He would comfort you and draw near to you as you draw near to Him.

Fortunately, the experience of feeling the full weight of sin is more than counterbalanced with the grace God has poured out toward you in His love and forgiveness. Brokenness and grieving over your sin will be the occasion for God to overwhelm you with His forgiveness and grace.

♥ What are your feelings about coming close to God and truly mourning your sin? (Are you perhaps frightened, angry, relieved, etc.?) Pour out your heart before our ever present and listening Lord.

Day 2
Scripture: Psalm 51:1-17

1 "Have mercy on me, O God, according to your unfailing love; according to your great compassion blot out my transgressions. 2 Wash away all my iniquity and cleanse me from my sin. 3 For I know my transgressions, and my sin is always before me. 4 Against you, you only, have I sinned and done what is evil in your sight, so that you are proved right when you speak and justified when you judge. 5 Surely I have been a sinner from birth, sinful from the time my mother conceived me. 6 Surely you desire truth in the inner parts; you teach me wisdom in the inmost place. 7 Cleanse me with hyssop, and I will be clean; wash me, and I will be whiter than snow. 8 Let me hear joy and gladness; let the bones you have crushed rejoice. 9 Hide your face from my sins and blot out all my iniquity. 10 Create in me a pure heart, O God, and renew a steadfast spirit within me. 11 Do not cast me from your presence or take your Holy Spirit from me. 12 Restore to me the joy of your salvation and grant me a willing spirit, to sustain me. 13Then I will teach transgressors your ways, and sinners will turn back to you. 14 Save me from bloodguilt, O God, the God who saves me, and my tongue will sing of your righteousness. 15 O Lord, open my lips, and my mouth will declare your praise. 16 You do not take delight in sacrifice, or I would bring it; you do not take pleasure in burnt offerings. 17 The sacrifices of God are a broken spirit; a broken and contrite heart, O God, you will not despise."

* Read verses 3 & 4 again. What words indicate that David "owns" his sin?

* Who does David say he sinned against?

At the heart of sin is rebellion against God; a refusal to obey Him as the Creator and Master of your life.

* Pray and confess to God that your abortion(s) was (were) sin.

Scripture: Psalm 51:1-17 Read these verses again.
☙ List all the requests David makes of God. For example, in the first verse, there are two: "have mercy on me" and "blot out my transgressions."

* Now take time to write out and pray each of David's requests for yourself, naming sins.

Scripture: I John 1:9
"If we confess our sins, He is faithful and just and will forgive us our sins and purify us from all unrighteousness."

* If you just confessed your sins, has God forgiven you?

* What words in this verse assure you that God forgives all sins?

Scripture: Psalm 103:11-12

"*For as high as the heavens are above the earth, so great is His love for those who fear Him; as far as the east is from the west, so far has He removed our transgressions from us.*"

♥ On the scale of 1-10, see below, where are you in having a deep assurance that you are completely and gloriously forgiven? (Draw a heart on the scale below, representing your answer.)

1————————————————————————————————————10

ashamed, guilty   *completely forgiven*

I hope you have experienced a deep assurance that you are completely and gloriously forgiven. Thank Him for His great mercy and love. If you still feel guilty, continue to petition God to bring that assurance to your heart.

Day 3
Scripture: Psalm 51:1-17 Read these verses one more time.

☙ Look for everything that David says about the nature or character of God. For example, in verse 1 he mentions God's unfailing love and great compassion. List all the others you can find.

* Take a few moments and thank God for who He is and for each of the character traits you have listed.

How has God forgiven you? Because God is loving and kind and merciful and just and generous and He was willing to die in your place. Make no mistake! Your appropriation of forgiveness doesn't depend on you in any way. God doesn't forgive you because you prayed loud enough, or you cried sincerely enough, or you did the right number of good things for others. His promise of forgiveness rests solely on His character. He is merciful. He is full of loving kindness toward you. He is gracious. REJOICE in His goodness toward you!

♥ Are you able to fully accept God's forgiveness based on His character and not your sorrow?

Day 4

Scripture: James 4:9

"Grieve, mourn and wail. Change your laughter to mourning and your joy to gloom."

The exhortations to grieve and mourn refer primarily to your response to sin. Hopefully, over the past two days, Psalm 51 and God's grace have helped you grieve over your sin of abortion. However, I think there is another application for this verse, namely, mourning the death of your baby(ies).

Scripture: Matthew 2:16-18

16*"When Herod realized that he had been outwitted by the Magi, he was furious, and he gave orders to kill all the boys in Bethlehem and its vicinity who were two years old and under, in accordance with the time he had learned from the Magi. 17 Then what was said through the prophet Jeremiah was fulfilled: 18 A voice is heard in Ramah, weeping and great mourning, Rachel weeping for her children and refusing to be comforted, because they are no more."*

* Who did Herod order to be killed?

↤ What was the response to the death of the children?

If you have never grieved over the child or children you aborted, allow yourself that time today. The truth is that you lost a real person. You will never hold that baby, or swing that toddler on a swing, or give that ten year old a birthday party or nag that teenager about picking up his/her room, etc.

* Are there reminders presently in your life that your child(ren) is (are) absent from you?

It is not wrong to be sad, to cry or whatever else you need to do to express your grief. But don't get lost in guilt and regrets! Bring all your emotions to your tender Father and pray for His comfort and touch.

Scripture: Psalm 147:3

"He heals the brokenhearted and binds up their wounds."

You might also want to do something special in memory of your dead child(ren). I planted a shrub in my yard in my child's memory; other women I know have written a letter or held a memorial service. You could involve other people or do something just between you and God.

❤ Share here what you would like to do in memory of your baby(ies).

Day 5

Genesis 18:25b says, *"Will not the Judge of all the earth do right?"* As this verse suggests, God is the judge of all who have died and this rhetorical question assures us that His judgment is right and completely just. What about aborted babies? Is (are) your baby(ies) in heaven? You will look at several Scriptures today with the goal of basing your assurance of heaven for your aborted child(ren) on biblical truth rather than wishful thinking.

Scripture: Psalm 51:5
    " Surely I was sinful at birth, sinful from the time my mother conceived me."

* Even from conception, what is true about babies?

Realize that "sinful" is speaking of the sin nature we all inherit because of Adam's original sin (see Romans 5:18). However, Jesus' death paid for Adam's sin, along with the sins of the world.

Scripture: Ezekiel 18:20a
    "The soul who sins is the one who will die. The son will not share the guilt of the father, nor will the father share the guilt of the son."

* What's the biblical principle taught in this verse?

* According to this principle, will your aborted baby (babies) be held responsible for your sin?

Please recall that if you have confessed abortion as sin before God and have asked His forgiveness, then you are no longer guilty before a righteous God. He has forgiven you!

Scripture: John 3:36
    "Whoever believes in the Son has eternal life, but whoever rejects the Son will not see life, for God's wrath remains on him."

* On what basis does a person obtain eternal life?

* Was your unborn child(ren) able to believe in Jesus?

Scripture: Revelation 20:12

"And I saw the dead great and small, standing before the throne, and books were opened. Another book was opened, which is the book of life. The dead were judged according to what they had done as recorded in the books."

* Besides unbelief (which excludes unbelievers from the book of life) what will people be judged by?

* Do unborn children commit any sins? Do they have any "works," good or bad?

To summarize thus far, aborted babies do not have the ability or opportunity to either reject Jesus (unbelief) or to sin. Their sin nature has been covered by Jesus' death on the cross. As with all of us, salvation is by grace alone (Ephesians 2:8-9). And how could God with His gracious, good, merciful and loving character not provide salvation for "innocent," unborn children?

Scripture: II Samuel 12: 21-23 (after David and Bathsheba's baby died, David bathed, worshiped and ate)

21"His servants asked him, 'Why are you acting this way? While the child was alive, you fasted and wept, but now that the child is dead, you get up and eat!' 22 He answered, 'While the child was still alive, I fasted and wept. I thought "Who knows? The Lord may be gracious to me and let the child live." 23 But now that he is dead, why should I fast? Can I bring him back again? I will go to him, but he will not return to me.' "

* How was David's response to his son's death unusual?

* Did he grieve or mourn after his baby died?

↤ Where does David say he'll go someday?

Contrast David's response to this son's death with how he responded to the death of Absalom, another of his sons.

Scripture: II Samuel 18:33; 19:1-2

33"The king was shaken. He went up to the room over the gateway and wept. As he went, he said: 'O my son Absalom! My son, my son Absalom! If only I had died instead of you–O Absalom, my son, my son!' "

1"Joab was told, 'The king is weeping and mourning for Absalom.' 2And for the whole army the victory that day was turned into mourning, because on that day the troops heard it said, 'The king is grieving for his son.' "

* How did David respond when he heard about Absalom's death?

↦ How different was this response from the manner in which David responded to his baby's death?

Absalom was a wicked person who had actually plotted against his father David. There is nothing in Scripture that indicates that Absalom repented or had faith in God, so we assume that his eternal fate was hell. It seems likely that David knew his infant was going to heaven and worshiped whereas he grieved because Absalom was going to hell.

♥ Having read and considered these Scriptures and biblical arguments, what do you believe about the eternal destiny of your aborted child(ren)?

MICHELLE

"What shall I render unto the LORD for all His benefits toward me? I will take the cup of salvation, and call upon the name of the LORD." Psalm 116:12-13

How can I repay the LORD for all that He has given me? I rejoice in the answer the psalmist gives, because it speaks of the abundant giving nature of God, for whom the greatest gift we can give is to receive, and to call on Him, to reach for Him, to accept from Him the water of life given freely as a gift, to drink from His cup.

For me, receiving salvation and forgiveness from God was both a one-time experience, starkly and unmistakably dividing a lost life from one that was redeemed, and is also an ongoing unfolding experience with ever-deepening levels of submission and reward.

Many years ago I had an abortion and I had an almost-abortion. These seemed necessary to sustain a lifestyle whose central motive was to "exercise my sexual freedom," in the words of the day, and to insulate my sexuality from consequence.

My world was shaken by the abortion, and God stepped forward to speak to me in a most unlikely way. As I left the abortion clinic, shattered by the brutality of the act I had just engaged in, through tears my eyes were drawn to a small metal button on the ground just next to my car door.

It was the kind of button you pin on your lapel, and this one looked like it had been driven over and trampled on for a decade or so. It pictured a mother bird sheltering baby birds under her wings, and singing the words, "He careth for you." Long before I was able to "take the cup of salvation" or "call upon the name of the LORD," I got my first instruction into His divine nature. Inasmuch as those four words were an invitation to receive comfort during that dark time, I took what was offered and began to lean on God.

Even then I was unable to conduct my life differently, and I soon became pregnant again and found myself in the waiting room of another abortion clinic. This time, however, something had changed. For one thing, there were ladies praying for me in a little huddle outside the clinic. I had done my best to ignore them as I came in.

The doctor was an hour behind schedule, by the mercy of God, and during that hour I found a willingness to give up my plans and make a place for this child in my life. Just as I was getting my $100 back from the receptionist, my boyfriend ran in hoping against hope that it wasn't too late, because his heart had undergone a change during that hour also.

I received my marriage proposal while driving away from an abortion clinic in Corpus Cristi, Texas, and this year I celebrate 28 years of marriage to the father of that precious son and a beloved daughter who completed our family.

Jesus teaches Peter that one who is forgiven much loves much. I am that one who has been forgiven much and I treasure the mercy and amazing saving grace I found in Jesus. But I couldn't look at my abortion without seeing the almost-abortion, because the child that came so close to perishing was born and grew to be a wonderful boy. He is a very gifted grad student at Yale Law School, happily married and the father of two beautiful children, and through his prayers, alongside those of my husband and daughter, I was emboldened to ask Jesus into my heart. Seeing my son's wonderful life was a stinging reminder of the potential that I came so close to destroying in him, and did destroy through the abortion.

Jesus offered me forgiveness for the abortion and the almost-abortion when He gave His life as the sacrificial Lamb of God that takes away the sin of the world. It took time even after coming to live for Him before I was able to receive the offered forgiveness, and truly dwell in a Kingdom free of condemnation. I judged my debt to be un-payable.

In preparing a teaching at my church on forgiveness, I came up with the following statement: "When we do not forgive, we place ourselves on the judge's bench instead of submitting to God's authority as judge. This is a form of vanity and idolizing the self that allows us to cling to the sweet savor of vengeance, instead of trusting that the Lord is a just and perfect judge. Vengeance, the Bible says, is the Lord's."

Was I willing to let go of the familiar old companion, the habitual self-condemnation? I learned something else about forgiveness in preparing to teach on it: choosing to forgive is an act of will. One day I made the choice to include my own name on the list of people I needed to forgive.

Then, as the Holy Spirit gave me insight, I further understood that Jesus' work of forgiveness is perfect, whole and complete, so that even questions of self-forgiveness began to fall away. Jesus forgave, and that was all that mattered.

There is no transgression too great to be forgiven by Jesus. If He is willing to forgive us, who are we to withhold forgiveness of ourselves?

What then shall I render unto the LORD for all His benefit toward me? I will acknowledge Him as the One who gives good and perfect things, and honor Him by receiving what He offers; I will take the cup of salvation. And I will acknowledge Him as the One who answers; I will call upon the name of the LORD.

"Casting all your care upon Him; for He careth for you." 1 Peter 5:7

Chapter Seven:
WASH YOUR HANDS: DEALING WITH ANGER

James 4:8b has two commands ("*wash your hands and purify your hearts*") and in this chapter we will look at the first one in some detail. In Scripture, the hands (or members) usually refer to external or visible things like our actions, speech, and attitudes particularly in relationship to other people.

While it may be true that other people have hurt you or sinned against you during your abortion experience(s), it is also true that you are responsible for your responses to others. To wash your hands means to cleanse yourself of any wrong actions and attitudes toward others including anger, bitterness, retaliation, verbal abuse, lack of forgiveness, etc. The goal in this chapter is to examine your life for anger and bitterness and in the next chapter you'll be asked to deal with these emotions by forgiving others who have sinned against you.

Day 1
* What's your definition of anger?

* With what or with whom were you angry at the time of your abortion(s)?

* Is there anyone toward whom you still feel anger?

♥ What did you do with your anger? How did you express it?

Anger is an emotion that God feels; there are many instances in the Old Testament in which God was angry with the nation of Israel. Observe the two Scriptures below:

Numbers 11:1
    "*Now the people complained about their hardships in the hearing of the Lord, and when He heard them His anger was aroused.*"

Numbers 11:10:
    "*Moses heard the people of every family wailing, each at the entrance to his tent. The Lord became exceedingly angry, and Moses was troubled.*"

* Think about this definition of anger (paraphrased from Dr. Tim Keller):
"Anger is a strong emotion which seeks to defend something good and to attack evil or injustice."

⤙ Does God's anger fit with this definition?

* Does your anger?

Day 2

Humans have many ways of expressing anger toward one another. Some people deny that they are angry and suppress it; some people give others the silent treatment; some blow up in a verbal tongue lashing while others become violent and physically abusive.

Scripture: Ephesians 4:26-27
   "In your anger do not sin: Do not let the sun go down while you are still angry, and do not give the devil a foothold."

⤙ What do these verses say to the person who thinks it is wrong for a Christian to be angry?

* Is it godly to feel anger but to suppress or stuff it?

* What does the phrase "do not let the sun go down..." suggest to you?

* From Ephesians 4:26-7, what's the danger in expressing anger in a sinful manner?

♥ How do you characteristically deal with your anger?

Day 3

  As you saw yesterday, it is not a sin to be angry. The possibility of sin comes in how the anger gets expressed. Today you will look at three sinful expressions of anger: *wrath, bitterness, and revenge.*

Scripture: James 1:19-20

  "My dear brothers, take note of this: Everyone should be quick to listen, slow to speak and slow to become angry, for a man's anger does not bring about the righteous life that God desires."

*The word angry and anger is also translated as "wrath." Look up *wrath* in the dictionary. Write out its definition:

* Have you ever experienced your anger as wrath?

* According to the verses in James, how is wrath related to righteousness?

Scripture: Hebrews 12:14-15

  "Make every effort to live in peace with all men and to be holy; without holiness no one will see the Lord. See to it that no one misses the grace of God and that no bitter root grows up to cause trouble and defile many."

  Bitterness can be defined as a continual hope for someone else's distress; you want the person who hurt you to get paid back.

* Where does a bitter spirit come from (Hebrews 12:14-15)?

*According to these verses, what's the consequence of bitterness?

Scripture: Romans 12:17-19

  "Do not repay anyone evil for evil. Be careful to do what is right in the eyes of everybody. If it is possible, as far as it depends on you, live at peace with everyone. Do not take revenge, my friends, but leave room for God's wrath, for it is written: 'It is mine to avenge; I will repay,' says the Lord."

* How is anger related to the desire for revenge?

* Are you a person who holds grudges? Do you ever tell others how you've been hurt to display the one who hurt you in a negative light?

↤ According to these three Scripture references, is wrath, bitterness or revenge an acceptable expression of anger?

When others have sinned against you and hurt you, you may have felt anger in response. As you saw, the emotion of anger in itself is not sinful. However, what you do with the anger or how it gets expressed is often sinful.

❤ Are you bitter or desiring revenge toward others connected with your abortion?

*Take time to pray and ask God's forgiveness for any sinful expressions of anger you have toward others in relation to your abortion(s).

Day 4

One truth that may be difficult to accept is that no person or situation <u>causes</u> you to express anger sinfully. In our language we speak as if there is a cause and effect relationship between people's actions and our sinful anger. We frequently say "so and so made me angry" as if anger was the inevitable response. Although it may seem spontaneous and unconscious, anger is a choice. When someone sins against you or stands in the way of something you desire, you do not have to express anger sinfully. Today you'll look at a few occasions when Jesus was angry. Notice what was happening in each situation and how He expressed His anger.

Scripture: Mark 3:1-6

"Another time he went into the synagogue, and a man with a shriveled hand was there. Some of them were looking for a reason to accuse Jesus, so they watched Him closely to see if He would heal him on the Sabbath. Jesus said to the man with the shriveled hand, 'Stand up in front of everyone.' Then Jesus asked them, 'Which is lawful on the Sabbath: to do good or to do evil, to save life or to kill?' But they remained silent. He looked around at them in anger, and deeply distressed at their stubborn hearts, said to the man, 'Stretch out your hand.' He stretched it out, and his hand was completely restored. Then the Pharisees went out and began to plot with the Herodians how they might kill Jesus."

* What made Jesus angry?

* How did He express His anger?

Scripture: Mark 10:13-16

"People were bringing little children to Jesus to have him touch them, but the disciples rebuked them. When Jesus saw this, He was indignant. He said to them, 'Let the little children come to me, and do not hinder them, for the kingdom of God belongs to such as these. I tell you the truth, anyone who will not receive the kingdom of God like a little child will never enter it.' And He took the children in his arms, put His hands on them and blessed them."

* What made Jesus angry?

* How did He express His anger?

Scripture: John 2:13-16

"When it was almost time for the Jewish Passover, Jesus went up to Jerusalem. In the temple courts He found men selling cattle, sheep and doves, and others sitting at tables exchanging money. So He made a whip out of cords, and drove all from the temple area, both sheep and cattle; he scattered the coins of the money changers and overturned their tables. To those who sold doves He said, 'Get these out of here! How dare you turn my Father's house into a market!' "

* What made Jesus angry?

* How did He express His anger?

❧ In the three passages you just read what is the link between anger and action?

* Was Jesus' anger ever expressed in a way that harmed people verbally or physically?

♥ With Jesus as your role model, how does your expression of anger need to change?

Day 5
Scripture: Psalm 4:4-5

    "In your anger do not sin; when you are on your beds, search your hearts and be silent. Offer right sacrifices and trust in the Lord."

⇛ What five things are you told to do when you are angry?

* Is it sinful to feel anger?

❤ When does anger become sin?

* When you are on your beds seems to refer to time when you aren't immersed in the conflict, but are alone and have time to reflect. What are you to do in this quiet time?

* What does it mean to search your heart?

* What does it mean to be silent?

    Have you ever noticed that when you're angry you rehearse to yourself and to others how the other person has wronged you? Your focus is on the other and that person is portrayed as the only wrong party who deserves severe punishment. But God would have you step back from that attitude (be silent) and think about your responses (search your heart).

* What would be a right sacrifice?

* Can you trust God to avenge the wrong committed against you?

    Think about those with whom you are still angry or bitter. Listen to God. What were you defending? Did you attack sin or a person? Put on the fruits of righteousness and repent. Trust God and do whatever He is asking you to do to make the broken relationship right. There is deep joy and healing when you are able to let go of anger and bitterness.

KIM

I was 18 yrs old, a senior in high school. I was in an abusive relationship that was going nowhere. I was a bright young girl, who knew better than to stay in that relationship, but was fearful of what he might do to me or himself if I left. That summer, I found myself pregnant. I had Christian friends, but was too ashamed to turn to them or my parents (who were not believers at the time). So I turned to a friend who had recently had an abortion. "She'll point me in the right direction and help me do what needs to be done," I told myself. Mainly, I was scared that if I had his child, it would tie me to him forever; I had always hoped for a way out, eventually. I met with a "counselor" from Planned Parenthood who asked me if anyone was forcing me to do this. "No!" was my quick answer. Then she asked why I wanted an abortion and my reply was, "Because I want to go to college next year and I'm just not ready for the responsibility." I wanted to say, "I'm scared to death of the father! He doesn't deserve this baby! I don't want to end up with him for the rest of my life!" She approved my answer and that was that. A couple of weeks later I came back for my appointment.

It was the absolute strangest day. I remember them giving me a room to change my clothes and then pointing me into the "waiting room." I sat on the floor with 12 other girls roughly my age, all in light blue gowns. We sat there, staring at the floor, at our hands, at the walls, ... careful not to make much eye contact with one another. They called for us one by one. When it was our turn, we walked into a room with a man holding the device to be inserted, a woman helping him, and a lady that was there to hold my hand and talk to me. I remember her saying that this was going to hurt a little, but it would all be over quickly. I asked, "How much will it hurt?" And she just said, "It will all be over quickly." I asked her if I could squeeze her hand and she said, "Certainly." It was horrible! It was loud! They told me to relax and be still so that he would get it all! I remember trembling, freezing and my heart about to pound out of my chest! Suddenly, it was over. They helped me into a large pad for bleeding and sat me in a "recovery room" to watch TV, eat tomato soup and drink some juice. Soon, it was time to go home and hope that my mother noticed nothing.

Where was the father? Oh, it was the week that everyone went to Myrtle Beach after graduation! He was at the beach with the current "girl of the week." He had saved and saved his money so that he could have a blast this spring break with all his buddies (and mine). He did borrow the money from a friend to pay for the abortion. I stayed home healing. I pushed this experience so far from my mind that I did not think about it, deal with it, or ever really consider it again until...

In June of 1997, I fell in love with my Savior, Jesus Christ. My husband and I were being trained as phone counselors for a follow up to Outreach Carolina, a huge evangelistic outreach in Charlotte, NC. I was reading and practically memorizing the tract, "Steps to Peace with God," when I realized that I did not have a personal relationship with Jesus Christ! I had never admitted that I needed Him to forgive me of my sins! Before then, I really never believed that Jesus was the only way! I knelt at the kitchen table with my husband and confessed my sins and my love for Christ and vowed to follow Him for the rest of my life. A few months later, we found ourselves in a great church with other believers, growing and being discipled. I was in the middle of a Beth Moore Bible study on David, I'll never forget the day. I awoke like always and went to the couch to do my Bible study about 6am. My husband left for work and I still sat there in my pajamas, studying. Twelve hours later, he walked in the door for dinner and I hadn't moved–same position studying, just as broken as ever! I was flooded with thoughts about FORGIVENESS! You mean I have to forgive those who have abused me? Those who have treated me horribly? Those who have taken advantage of me sexually and robbed me of my innocence? I couldn't imagine that my Savior loved them as much as He loved me!!! How could that be? They don't DESERVE it! Then...I remembered... my abortion. I thought to myself, "Oh God, not me! Did I really do that? I now believe that life begins at conception and that You and only You give life. Did I really end a LIFE?"

A couple of months went by and I had to study, pray and talk, talk, talk... I had to realize and understand the depths of God's love for me! I had to learn to forgive those who had offended me! It was freeing when I did. But, then came the tougher part of forgiving myself for my own sins and realizing that it wasn't ME doing the forgiving, but Christ Himself! If Christ's shed blood wasn't enough for my sin, then His very death is a mockery!

Today, I have a sweet peace and unbelievable assurance that I do have a child at the feet of Jesus in Heaven. If you are recovering from making a decision to have an abortion—you do too! I may not understand it all, but my faith carries me through. I have been forgiven and my Heavenly Father sees only the blood of Christ Jesus when He looks down upon me. His grace and mercy sustain me. Is it occasionally hard? Of course, there are memories that come and go. But, overall, it's a reminder of how much I TRULY NEED a Savior and I'm forever grateful.

Chapter Eight:
WASH YOUR HANDS: FORGIVENESS

Forgiveness is a very important and perhaps surprising part of your healing. You have already looked at Scriptures that talk about God's forgiveness of you, but you also need to look at forgiveness within your horizontal relationships.

Because you have a sin nature, you sin. You do and say things that hurt or offend others and other people do and say things that hurt you. Often sins that are committed against one another break or damage relationships. For example, the sinful expressions of anger you read about last chapter can result in broken relationships. Forgiveness is the element that restores relationships.

God's overarching principle for our horizontal relationships with others is to be at peace with everyone. The goal of this chapter is to help you learn how to seek forgiveness when you have wronged someone else, and how to respond biblically when someone has wronged you. The consequence of following God's principles of forgiveness is that you will experience healing in your relationships with others.

Day 1

During your abortion experience(s), have you identified people that you sinned against in either word or deed? Name them and the sin(s).

Scripture: Psalm 51:3-4

"For I know my transgressions, and my sin is always before me. Against you, you only, have I sinned and done what is evil in your sight, so that you are proved right when you speak and justified when you judge."

* How is your sin against another person related to sin against God?

Scripture: Matthew 5:23-24

"Therefore, if you are offering your gift at the altar and there remember that your brother has something against you, leave your gift there in front of the altar. First go and be reconciled to your brother; then come and offer your gift."

❧ What should you do when you have sinned against another?

If you have sinned against another, ask for God's forgiveness first. Then ask the individual(s) that you have offended for forgiveness. The words to use in seeking forgiveness are very important. You should name the particular sin(s) and ask the person to forgive you. If necessary, you should make restitution. Note: apologizing is not the same thing as asking for forgiveness. Saying you are sorry just tells how you feel. It does not show that you own the sin and are truly repentant for it.

For example, in my own life, I made the decision to abort. When I discovered that I was pregnant, I had called up the father of the child and told him about it, but I disregarded his feelings and he had no say in the decision. After I became a Christian and wanted to clean my slate with him, I spoke to him and said something like "I want to ask for your forgiveness because I know that I was wrong when I told you I was going to abort our child. I didn't even give you a chance to say anything and I ignored your feelings. That was wrong of me. Will you forgive me for how badly I treated you?" I also asked him if I had done other things that had offended or hurt him and I asked forgiveness for those things as well.

It was very hard to humble myself before him and admit that I did wrong, but it was worth it! I can't tell you the joyous feeling I experienced when that burden was lifted off of me and I was right with him.

♥ Is there someone whom you need to go and seek forgiveness? Write out what you might say.

Day 2

Typical responses to being sinned against include anger and bitterness. Last chapter you saw that these are not godly. So how should you respond when you've been hurt by someone else's sin?

Scripture: Colossians 3:13

"Bear with each other and forgive whatever grievances you may have against one another. Forgive as the Lord forgave you."

❧ What does it mean to bear with one another?

This verse encourages you to overlook offenses and annoyances. This is not a denial of the sins or faults of others. You aren't trying to pretend that someone's words or actions didn't hurt. And you shouldn't think that somehow you deserve to be sinned against. Instead, by God's grace, you choose to overlook the offense or complaint against another person.

Were some of the hurts you received minor? Were you perhaps hypersensitive to a thoughtless comment or action? Did you take up an offense when it would have been just as easy to overlook it? Ask God to help you sort through the situations of hurt and determine which were minor.

Scripture: Psalm 62:8
"Trust in Him at all times, O people; pour out your hearts to him, for God is our refuge."

* What is a refuge?

♥ What is God inviting you to do with your hurts?

As you read the Scriptures over the next three days, keep Jay Adams' definition of forgiveness in mind. He writes, "Forgiveness is the promise not to raise the issue again to the offender, to others, or to himself."

Day 3
Scripture: Matthew 6:14-15
"For if you forgive men when they sin against you, your heavenly Father will also forgive you. But if you do not forgive men their sins, your Father will not forgive your sins."

* How seriously does God view this matter of forgiving others?

Scripture: Matthew 18: 21-22
"Then Peter came to Jesus and asked, 'Lord, how many times shall I forgive my brother when he sins against me? Up to seven times?'"
"Jesus answered, 'I tell you, not seven times, but seventy-seven times.'"

* Is there a limit to how often we forgive others?

Scripture: Ephesians 4:32

"Be kind and compassionate to one another, forgiving each other, just as in Christ God forgave you."

* State the two exhortations found in this verse.

Scripture: Luke 23:34a

"Jesus said, 'Father, forgive them, for they do not know what they are doing.' "

* Did those who crucified Jesus repent and ask for forgiveness?

* Did they deserve to be forgiven?

Scripture: Jeremiah 31:34a

"For I will forgive their wickedness and will remember their sins no more."

* What does God mean when He says He will remember sin no more? Does God literally forget the sin?

⤙ Summarize what these Bible passages teach about forgiveness.

♥ Why is it difficult to forgive those who have hurt us?

Day 4

Scripture: Matthew 18: 23-35

23"Therefore, the kingdom of heaven is like a king who wanted to settle accounts with his servants. 24 As he began the settlement, a man who owed him ten thousand talents was brought to him. 25 Since he was not able to pay, the master ordered that he and his wife and his children and all that he had be sold to repay the debt. 26 The servant fell on his knees before him. 'Be patient with me,' he begged, 'and I will pay back everything.' 27 The servant's master took pity on him, canceled the debt and let him go. 28 But when that servant went out, he found one of his fellow servants who owed him a hundred denarii. He grabbed him and began to choke him, 'Pay back what you owe me!' he demanded. 29 His fellow servant fell to his knees and begged him, 'Be patient with me, and I will pay you back.' 30 But he refused. Instead, he went off and had the man thrown into prison until he could pay the debt. 31 When the other servants saw what had happened, they were greatly distressed *and went and told their master everything that had happened. 32 Then the master called the servant in. 'You wicked servant,' he said, 'I canceled all that debt of yours because you begged me to. 33 Shouldn't you have had mercy on your fellow servant just as I had on you?' 34 In anger his master turned him over to the jailers until he should pay back all he owed. 35 This is how my heavenly Father will treat each of you unless you forgive your brother from your heart."*

ᗡ What principles about forgiveness is Jesus teaching in this parable?
(in particular, see verses 32-33)

* What role does mercy play in forgiveness?

*Picture a seesaw. On one side is the debt you owe God. On the other is the debt another person owes you. Which side is heavier?

* Did the first servant "feel" like forgiving the debt his fellow servant owed him?

Scripture: Mark 11:25 (Jesus is speaking)
"And when you stand praying, if you hold anything against anyone, forgive him, so that your Father in heaven may forgive you your sins."

* Does God tell you to wait until you "feel" like forgiving?

♥ Write down specific sins and individuals God is prompting you to forgive.

Day 5
Assuming that you choose to forgive the person who hurt you, now what do you do? The human tendency is to withdraw from the offending party and avoid him or her. One action God may ask you to take involves confrontation.

Scripture: Matthew 18:15
"If your brother sins against you, go and show him his fault, just between the two of you. If he listens to you, you have won your brother over."

Scripture: Luke 17:3

 "So watch yourselves. If your brother sins, rebuke him, and if he repents, forgive him."

* What is the instruction in both these passages?

↬ What is the goal of confrontation when someone has sinned against you?

Scripture: Ephesians 4:15

 "Instead, speaking the truth in love, we will in all things grow up into Him who is the Head, that is, Christ."

♥ What's the correct attitude to have when you confront another about his/her sin that hurt you?

Confronting someone who has sinned against you gives that individual an opportunity to repent and to ask your forgiveness. If he/she repents and does ask your forgiveness, then you verbally grant forgiveness and the relationship gets a clean slate. However, if your confrontation is not received in the way you intended, then you must still extend the willingness to forgive in your heart. If the offense is serious and should not be overlooked, it may need to be brought to the church leadership (see Matthew 18: 16-17).

How do you know when you should confront and when you should forgive in your heart and be silent? This is a matter in which you need God's wisdom. James 1:5 states, *"If any of you lacks wisdom, he should ask God, who gives generously to all without finding fault, and it will be given to him."* Remember the goal of confrontation is to restore the relationship that has been broken by sin. If your heart motives aren't right or if the other person is not a believer and won't understand, it may be wiser to keep quiet. But if the other person is a believer, then your confrontation is providing an opportunity for him or her to make things right with God and you.

Review the different principles you've studied and decide with God's help, what you need to do. And then... *"Be ye doers of the word"*...(James 1:22).

DEB

How does it feel to carry a secret for 19 years? What is it like when that secret takes on a life of its own and begins to tear a person apart from the inside out? Unbearable. Agonizing. Damaging. But believe it or not, I didn't even know it was happening.

Ever since I was 13 years old, I had dreamed of going to Bible College and becoming a missionary. I grew up in a Christian home and I loved the Lord Jesus with all my heart. And I was absolutely sure that I would wait until marriage before having a sexual relationship! Having a real steady boyfriend my senior year of high school was intoxicating. When he and I started going steady, I made it clear that we were not going to have a sexual relationship. He said that he understood and that he wouldn't pressure me. But as we spent more and more time together, the desire to make love was stronger than my resolve to wait and we began a sexual relationship.

What I wasn't prepared for was the devastating result in my spiritual life. I was living two lives! Still attending church and professing a Christian life, I was secretly carrying on a relationship with someone who did not believe in Christ. This was the beginning of an elaborate web of lies and cover-up that began to eat away at me from the inside out. After graduation, we broke up and I headed off to attend college.

In college, I began to explore life in the world–drinking with my friends and trying marijuana. I knew that my relationship with God was on the rocks and I tried to get back to what I once had but I really didn't know how. I became more and more involved in the weekend party scene. During a break, a male friend from my high school days invited me to get together for New Year's Eve. During that date, we became intimate...then, I became pregnant. Pregnant: that awful word. What could I do? Who could I talk to? I was alone, guilty, caught, exposed. What would people think? What would Mom and Dad think? Looking back, it's amazing how short the path was from the school clinic to the abortion clinic. Abortion seemed the only logical choice and it was seemingly effortless to go to the clinic and be processed through in just a couple of hours. Soon, I was back at school in high gear with my lifestyle of sex, drugs and rock and roll.

The following summer, I was suddenly taken very ill and whisked off to a hospital. Our family doctor had to do an emergency procedure because I had pelvic inflammatory disease (PID). Of course, my parents were very worried and wanted to know what was wrong and the doctor gave us some vague explanation that this happens from time to time. I was numb emotionally; nothing seemed to be a big deal. I recovered quickly that summer and decided to drop out of college. I got a restaurant job and continued my lifestyle of dangerous behaviors. My choices only resulted in more problems. I met a chef, and soon we were living together. In just a few months he asked me to marry him and I felt a flash of emotion, thinking maybe someone does love me. In a brief moment of insight I told my sister that getting married was the worst thing I could do, but I went ahead and got married. The following winter I became ill and once again was rushed to the hospital. This time I had to undergo a complete hysterectomy. My doctor told us that after my abortion, an infection had developed that resulted in the initial PID and its recurrence. I would never be able to have children. I was numb. I was still in complete denial regarding the consequences of abortion.

Our marriage lasted 4 years, and during that time was fraught with turmoil, lies and disappointment. We separated one summer after my husband attacked me in a jealous rage. I have never seen him since.

For the next few years, I made a decent living, shared a nice apartment with friends, but the weekends were still a time to party and continue with casual sex as a substitute for dealing with the utter chaos of emotion beneath the surface. I failed constantly in my resolve to get rid of the things that I used to cover my pain.

I began to hang out in Christian bookstores in order to try to feel like I was close to God. One day, I opened Roy Hession's book, *Calvary Road*. With amazement, I found the answer that I needed. I read that there was nothing that I could do to get good enough to please God and make Him forgive me. It reminded me of what I had learned as a child–that God wants me to come to Him as I am. As I made my humble confession, He was able to transform me. Soon, God used another book to help me deal with the issue of forgiveness. I realized that the hurts over all of the years–the drug use, the promiscuity and the wrong choices had been literally eating me up inside. I spent an entire afternoon letting God bring to my remembrance dozens of events, names, faces and acts that I had experienced in the nine years since my abortion. Under His guidance I was able to take responsibility and to give and receive forgiveness for the many sins of my life. God's peace and light came flowing into my soul!

Since that time, God has given me an amazing journey of restoration. I attended a Bible College, restoring the dream I had at age thirteen. After that I found myself the director of a new Crisis Pregnancy Center. It was at the center that I was finally able to tell my deeply buried secret. On the day of the official opening of the center, I had invited my parents to come. After we toured through the center and all of the other visitors had left, I knew I should speak. My parents were completely quiet as I told them about those days long ago when I faced a very difficult decision and chose to have an abortion. I told them how ashamed I was of what I had done and that my fear of how they would react had tormented me for many years. I asked for their forgiveness. Without missing a heartbeat, they drew me into their arms and said that I was their daughter and that there was nothing I could do for which they would not forgive me. They were so very sorry I had gone through such a difficult time alone and they told me they would be there for me in the future.

My joy and the forgiveness I experienced were indescribable! My secret was gone; it had lifted from me and risen up to the heavens to find a place in the hands of God and I was free.

Chapter Nine:
PURIFY YOUR HEARTS

In a previous chapter you looked at the command to cleanse your hands which lead to studies on anger and forgiveness. In this chapter you'll look at the second half of James 4:8b which says, "purify your hearts, you double-minded." The goal of this chapter is to look more deeply into the motives and heart desires that were involved in your abortion(s).

Day 1

The command to "purify your hearts, you double-minded" applies to all of us because we are of two minds; we vacillate between living for ourselves and living in obedience to God. This command calls for change below the surface; the heart represents your inner person which includes your beliefs, desires and motives. Because there is a powerful relationship between the heart and external sins, obedience to the command to purify your heart will result in changes in attitudes and behavior.

Scripture: Matthew 15:18-19

"But the things that come out of the mouth come from the heart, and these make a man 'unclean.' For out of the heart come evil thoughts, murder, adultery, sexual immorality, theft, false testimony, slander."

* How are your words related to your heart?

* List all the sins that come out of the heart.

Scripture: Luke 6:43-45:

"No good tree bears bad fruit, nor does a bad tree bear good fruit. Each tree is recognized by its own fruit. People do not pick figs from thorn bushes, or grapes from briers. The good man brings good things out of the good stored up in his heart, and the evil man brings evil things out of the evil stored up in his heart. For out of the overflow of his heart his mouth speaks."

* What's the relationship between your actions or words and your heart?

* If you represent the tree and your words and behavior are the fruit, then what is the root (origin) of the fruit?

↞ In both the previous passages, what is being identified as the source or origin of sin?

In order to purify your heart, you must first know what's going on in it. What are its hidden motives, beliefs and desires?

Scripture: Hebrews 4:12-13
    "The word of God is living and active. Sharper than any double-edged sword, it penetrates even to dividing soul and spirit, joints and marrow; it judges the thoughts and attitudes of the heart. Nothing in all creation is hidden from God's sight. Everything is uncovered and laid bare before the eyes of Him to whom we must give account."

* What is the Word of God able to do?

* Is God aware of what's going on in your heart?

Scripture: Psalm 139:23a
    "Search me, O God, and know my heart;..."

* Pray and ask God to help you understand your heart and to discern your inner motives and thoughts.

♥ What areas of your heart are not yet right with God?

Day 2
    Designed by God to be worshipers, I believe that our hearts are always actively involved in worship.

Scripture: Rom 1:25
    "They exchanged the truth of God for a lie, and worshiped and served created things rather than the Creator—who is forever praised. Amen."

* What are the two possible objects of our worship?

* What are some created things that capture your heart? Possibilities might include comfort, pleasure, being accepted by others, being regarded highly by others, control, money, status, etc.

Scripture: Jeremiah 17:9
> *"The heart is deceitful above all things and beyond cure. Who can understand it?"*

⌇ What is true about your heart?

If you are honest with God and yourself, you must admit that your heart is most often motivated by self. Abortion is a fruit that points to a selfish desire or motive in your heart.

♥ Take some time right now to reflect back on your abortion(s). What were the hidden desires of your heart? What were your motives? What unbelief was in your heart? How did you not trust God?

*Take a moment and confess to God your unseen heart sins that lead to abortion.

Scripture: Romans 7:24-25
> *"What a wretched man I am! Who will rescue me from this body of death? Thanks be to God—through Jesus Christ our Lord!"*

* Give God thanks that through Jesus Christ your heart sins have also been forgiven!

Day 3
Scripture: Psalm 24:3-4
> *"Who may ascend the hill of the Lord? Who may stand in His holy place? He who has clean hands and a pure heart, who does not lift up his soul to an idol or swear by what is false."*

* According to these verses who may be in the presence of God?

Having a pure heart implies a single-mindedness or single focus. When gold is pure, it contains only gold. When your heart is pure, only God is God. There are no idols in the heart. Think of an idol as anything or anyone that we desire, worship or serve instead of God Himself. Idols may not be obvious because they reside in the heart or inner person.

Scripture: Romans 1:21-25

"For although they knew God, they neither glorified Him as God nor gave thanks to Him, but their thinking became futile and their foolish hearts were darkened. Although they claimed to be wise, they became fools and exchanged the glory of the immortal God for images made to look like mortal man and birds and animals and reptiles. Therefore God gave them over in the sinful desires of their hearts to sexual impurity for the degrading of their bodies with one another. They exchanged the truth of God for a lie, and worshiped and served created things rather than the Creator—who is forever praised. Amen."

* Write out the exchanges that take place in sinners. The first is an exchange of the glory of God for images of created things. What are the other two exchanges?

* How do these verses relate to idolatry?

♥ Instead of believing the truth of God, what lies have you believed?

Scripture: Revelation 4:8-10

"Each of the four living creatures had six wings and was covered with eyes all around, even under his wings. Day and night they never stop saying: 'Holy, holy, holy is the Lord God Almighty, who was, and is, and is to come.' Whenever the living creatures give glory, honor and thanks to Him who sits on the throne and who lives for ever and ever, the twenty-four elders fall down before Him who sits on the throne, and worship Him who lives for ever and ever."

* The created beings who are in God's presence have pure hearts. What is their main activity in heaven?

Scripture: Psalm 119:9, 11 & 34

9 "How can a young man keep his way pure? By living according to your word."
11 "I have hidden your word in my heart that I might not sin against you."
34 "Give me understanding, and I will keep your law and obey it with all my heart."

✎ What is the connection between a pure heart and God's word?

Scripture: Psalm 51:10
"Create in me a pure heart, O God, and renew a steadfast spirit within me."

* Ask the Almighty Creator to create in you a new heart. Ask that He change your heart from one that is selfish to selfless; from one that serves self to a heart that serves God alone.

Day 4

As God changes your heart and you cooperate by renewing your mind with Scripture and by being obedient, the sinful nature progressively gets squeezed out. Worship of God and a desire to serve Him grows as you feed the new nature you've been given. A pure or single-minded heart is filled with one person–God. And just as sinful deeds and words come from your corrupt heart, good fruits come from a pure heart. There are all types of good fruit but you are going to concentrate on fruit that addresses specific issues from your abortion(s). If you have genuinely cleansed your hands and purified your heart, then good fruits should be beginning to develop. These include:

1) A deeper knowledge of God and who He is.

Scripture: Colossians 1:9-12.
   "For this reason, since the day we heard about you, we have not stopped praying for you and asking God to fill you with the knowledge of His will through all spiritual wisdom and understanding. And we pray this in order that you may live a life worthy of the Lord and may please Him in every way: bearing fruit in every good work, growing in the knowledge of God, being strengthened with all power according to His glorious might so that you may have great endurance and patience, and joyfully giving thanks to the Father who has qualified you to share in the inheritance of the saints in the kingdom of light."

✎ Dissect this prayer to discover seven things Paul is praying for the Colossians. For example, the first is that "God would fill them with the knowledge of His will."

* Pray this prayer for yourself.

2) A change in lifestyle.

Scripture: I Thessalonians 4:3-5.
"*It is God's will that you should be holy; that you should avoid sexual immorality; that each of you should learn to control his own body in a way that is holy and honorable, not in passionate lust like the heathen, who do not know God;*"

* Have you ended any pre- or extra-marital sexual relationships?

♥ What other changes in your life have you made in response to God's command to be holy?

3) Forgiveness–accepted and extended to others.

Scripture: Colossians 3:13.
"*Bear with each other and forgive whatever grievances you may have against one another. Forgive as the Lord forgave you.*"

*How has accepting God's forgiveness through Christ impacted your life?

*Have you asked for forgiveness from others you have hurt?

*Have you forgiven others who have hurt you?

Day 5
Today we will look at three additional fruits that are the result of a pure heart.

1) Goodness beyond forgiveness.

Scripture: Luke 6:35-36.
"*But love your enemies, do good to them, and lend to them without expecting to get anything back. Then your reward will be great, and you will be sons of the Most High, because He is kind to the ungrateful and wicked. Be merciful, just as your Father is merciful.*"

♥ What good things could you do to those who hurt or offended you in your abortion experience?

2) Ministry to others.

Scripture: II Corinthians 1:3-5.
"*Praise be to the God and Father of our Lord Jesus Christ, the Father of compassion and the God of all comfort, who comforts us in all our troubles, so that we can comfort those in any trouble with the comfort we ourselves have received from God. For just as the sufferings of Christ flow over into our lives, so also through Christ our comfort overflows.*"

*Have you been willing to comfort others? It doesn't have to be someone else who has had an abortion. Anyone who is hurting could use the comfort and encouragement that God has shown you. Are there verses that ministered to you that you have ready to share?

3) A sense of healing and purpose.

Scripture: Romans 8:28-29
"*And we know that in all things God works for the good of those who love Him, who have been called according to His purpose. For those God foreknew He also predestined to be conformed to the likeness of His Son, that He might be the firstborn among many brothers.*"

☞ How can God use even abortion to conform a woman to the image of Christ?

Scripture: Joel 2:25a
"*I will repay you for the years the locusts have eaten...*"

* Think of the locusts as the consequences of sin. What is God's promise in this verse?

If you don't see bushels of fruit, don't despair. As long as you seek God and trust Him, fruit is guaranteed.

Jeremiah 17:7-8 says...
"*But blessed is the man who trusts in the LORD, whose confidence is in Him. He will be like a tree planted by the water, that sends out its roots by the stream. It does not fear when heat comes; its leaves are always green. It has no worries in a year of drought, and never fails to bear fruit.*"

CHERIE

"Cover their faces with shame so that men will seek your name, O LORD."
Psalm 83:16

When I was a teen I made some very wrong choices. Choices which I didn't realize at the time would adversely affect my life. In fact, these choices would almost cost me my life! It all began with my desire to be loved and accepted–to be loved simply for who I was. But unfortunately, I looked for that love in all the wrong places.

At sixteen I found myself alone, afraid, and pregnant. I didn't know where to turn; I didn't know what to do. But conveniently located down the street from my high school was a clinic which told me, "Your secret is safe with us. No one will ever need to know. You can have a simple procedure done and your problem will be taken care of." I chose to believe their lies–and I had an abortion.

Soon my life was out of control. I tried to numb the pain with alcohol and when that no longer worked, I turned to drugs. Needless to say, my life was out of control. Still trying to find love in all the wrong places I ended up pregnant again at 18. I again chose abortion. No one ever told me the heartache I would feel. No one ever told me that I would want to destroy my life because I could no longer live with myself. NO ONE EVER TOLD ME!

But God in His love, grace, and mercy began to heal my broken heart. He used the guilt and the shame of my sin to draw me to Him with His loving-kindness. I had nowhere else to turn. He began to teach me how to give my deep heart hurts to Him. He taught me how to replace the hurt in my heart with His love and truth. And He began to mold me and make me into the woman He desires me to be.

As this transformation took place in my life, He called me to begin a ministry to help other women–to help their hearts be healed, like mine was, over the issue of abortion. It is amazing how God can take our most awful guilt and shame and turn it around to use it for His glory. He is an awesome God!

Since 1993 God has allowed me to be a part of His work in the lives of literally thousands of women, both in the States and in Eastern Europe. Women whose lives were touched as they learned how much God loves them and forgives them for the wrong choices they have made. Women whose lives were touched as they made right choices to give life to their babies. Women whose lives were touched as they learned more and more about Jesus and learned how to become all that He intends them to be.

It is absolutely amazing how God can take the ashes of our lives and use them for His glory.

God uses the guilt and the shame in our lives to draw us to Him. He wants to set us free. He wants us to become all that He intends us to be, so that we can reflect His glory. When we allow Him to transform our lives it is amazing. We transform from one whose face is covered with shame to one whose face is unveiled as we reflect His glory. This transformation can only take place as we allow God to heal our broken heart. As we do, *1 Corinthians 3:18* becomes true in our lives.

> *"And we, who with unveiled faces all reflect the Lord's glory, are being transformed into his likeness with ever-increasing glory, which comes from the Lord, who is the Spirit."*

Won't you allow Him to do His gentle surgery on your broken heart today? As you do, your face will no longer be covered by shame.

Chapter Ten:
HUMBLE YOURSELF IN THE SIGHT OF THE LORD

The final command found in *James 4:10 says, "Humble yourselves before the Lord, and He will lift you up."* Initially this command seems nearly identical to the command to submit to God. However, I think there is a subtle difference. Submission has to do with obedience and visible behaviors. It involves the authority structure of the world; God is the Creator and as His creature, you are to obey Him. The command to be humble addresses your internal attitudes–do you accept His authority? Do you understand the true nature of yourself and God? After all, God is not just your authority positionally; He is completely superior to you in His person. He is the most excellent, most perfect Being that exists! Humility is that inward disposition that stands in awe of who He is; falls before Him in recognition of who you are; and bows down in gratitude for what He has done for you.

The goal of this chapter is for you to grasp more fully who God is, and who you are in relation to Him. A correct understanding and humble demeanor results in true worship and amazingly, He promises blessing to the humble.

Day 1
Scripture: Proverbs 29:23
> *"A man's pride brings him low, but a man of lowly spirit gains honor."*

* What principle is taught in this verse?

Scripture: Isaiah 57:15
> *"For this is what the high and lofty One says—He who lives forever, whose name is holy: 'I live in a high and holy place, but also with him who is contrite and lowly in spirit, to revive the spirit of the lowly and to revive the heart of the contrite.' "*

* How is God identified in this verse?

* What kind of person is in God's presence?

↦ How does this verse relate to the principle found in Proverbs 29:23?

Scripture: I Peter 5:5-6

      "Young men, in the same way be submissive to those who are older. Clothe yourselves with humility toward one another, because, 'God opposes the proud but gives grace to the humble.' Humble yourselves, therefore, under God's mighty hand, that He may lift you up in due time."

* How does God respond to those who are humble?

❤ How would you describe your attitude toward God? Is it humble?

Day 2
Scripture: Matthew 11:28-29

      "Come to me, all you who are weary and burdened, and I will give you rest. Take my yoke upon you and learn from me, for I am gentle and humble in heart, and you will find rest for your souls."

* How does Jesus describe Himself?

Scripture: Mark 10:45

      "For even the Son of Man did not come to be served, but to serve, and to give His life as a ransom for many."

* Although Jesus was God and had a right to set himself up as Lord and King over all, what was his attitude?

Scripture: Philippians 2:6-8

      "Who, being in very nature God, did not consider equality with God something to be grasped, but made Himself nothing, taking the very nature of a servant, being made in human likeness. And being found in appearance as a man, He humbled himself and became obedient to death–even death on a cross!"

* In His very essence, who was Jesus?
* How did Christ live out the command in James 4:10 *("Humble yourselves before the Lord.")*

❥ How is humility related to obedience to God?

♥ Is your life reflecting the humility that Christ exhibits? How is He calling you to serve others?

Day 3
Scripture: Romans 12:3-5
"For by the grace given me I say to every one of you: Do not think of yourself more highly than you ought, but rather think of yourself with sober judgment, in accordance with the measure of faith God has given you. Just as each of us has one body with many members, and these members do not all have the same function, so in Christ we who are many form one body, and each member belongs to all the others...."

♥ What do you think it means to think of yourself with sober judgment?

Scripture: Luke 18: 9-14
9 "To some who were confident of their own righteousness and looked down on everybody else, Jesus told this parable: 10 'Two men went up to the temple to pray, one a Pharisee and the other a tax collector. 11 The Pharisee stood up and prayed about himself; "God, I thank you that I am not like all other men–robbers, evildoers, adulterers–or even like this tax collector. 12 I fast twice a week and give a tenth of all I get."

13 'But the tax collector stood at a distance. He would not even look up to heaven, but beat his breast and said, "God, have mercy on me, a sinner."

14 'I tell you that this man, rather than the other, went home justified before God. For everyone who exalts himself will be humbled, and he who humbles himself will be exalted.' "

* To whom did Jesus address this parable (verse 9)?

⊷ How does God respond to the person who humbles himself?

Scripture: II Corinthians 3:1-6
"Are we beginning to commend ourselves again? Or do we need, like some people, letters of recommendation to you or from you? You yourselves are our letter, written on our hearts, known and read by everybody. You show that you are a letter from Christ, the result of our ministry, written not with ink but with the Spirit of the living God, not on tablets of stone but on tablets of human hearts.

Such confidence as this is ours through Christ before God. Not that we are competent to claim anything for ourselves, but our competence comes from God. He has made us competent as ministers of a new covenant–not of the letter but of the Spirit; for the letter kills, but the Spirit gives life."

* Whose ministry was responsible for the salvation of the Corinthians?

* How did Paul view his ability to minister and win people to Christ?

* Are you humble enough before others to share your abortion story if God leads you to do so?

* During the past three days you have read several Scriptures dealing with humility. Write down any new insights you have received.

Day 4

Did you notice that all the verses that command you to humble yourself also promise you that God will lift you up?

James 4:10 "Humble yourselves before the Lord, and He will lift you up."

Proverbs 29:23 "A man's pride brings him low, but a man of lowly spirit gains honor."

I Peter 5:6 "Humble yourselves, therefore, under God's mighty hand, that He may lift you up in due time."

Matt 23:12 "For whoever exalts himself will be humbled, and whoever humbles himself will be exalted."

Scripture: Philippians 2:8-9
    "And being found in appearance as a man, He humbled himself and became obedient to death–even death on a cross! Therefore God exalted Him to the highest place and gave Him the name that is above every name..."

↬ As a result of Christ's humility and obedience, how has God exalted Him?

* Look back over all these verses. When you humble yourself, what does God do?

These promises (to be lifted up, honored, exalted), once again demonstrate how God's ways are not our ways. It is by humbling yourself that you are lifted up; it is by losing your life that you gain it. Humbling yourself goes against your pride; it goes against that spirit of independence and autonomy. In your human reasoning you may feel like humbling yourself to God will result in a life out of control. Indeed, it will be out of your control and placed in the hands of the One True God, who is fully Sovereign and absolutely Good.

♥ Will you trust Him in humility?

♥ What does humbling yourself look like?

Day 5

How do you or I cultivate true humility? It is an attitude that must be pursued and encouraged. As you meditate upon and experience who God is a humble spirit will grow in you.

Scripture: Romans 1:19-20

"...since what may be known about God is plain to them, because God has made it plain to them. For since the creation of the world God's invisible qualities–His eternal power and divine nature–have been clearly seen, being understood from what has been made, so that men are without excuse."

* What does the natural world reveal about the nature of God?

* Take time today to observe closely some part of God's creation (a bird, a flower, clouds, a landscape, etc.) and think about the creative and wise mind that thought of each detail of every created thing. Contemplate the awesome power that He displayed when He brought the created world into existence.

Scripture: Isaiah 6:1-7

"In the year that King Uzziah died, I saw the Lord seated on a throne, high and exalted, and the train of his robe filled the temple. Above him were seraphs, each with six wings; With two wings they covered their faces, with two they covered their feet, and with two they were flying. And they were calling to one another: 'Holy, holy, holy is the Lord Almighty; the whole earth is full of His glory.' At the sound of their voices the doorposts and thresholds shook and the temple was filled with smoke. 'Woe to me!' I cried. 'I am ruined! For I am a man of unclean lips, and I live among a people of unclean lips, and my eyes have seen the King, the Lord Almighty.' Then one of the seraphs flew to me with a live coal in his hand, which he had taken with tongs from the altar. With it he touched my mouth and said, 'See, this has touched your lips; your guilt is taken away and your sin atoned for.' "

* Describe Isaiah's vision of God.

* What is his response to seeing God in His glory?

☛ What makes it possible for Isaiah to remain in God's presence?

* How is your vision and knowledge of God related to the cultivation of humility?

Scripture: Colossians 1:15-20

"He is the image of the invisible God, the firstborn over all creation. For by Him all things were created: things in heaven and on earth, visible and invisible, whether thrones or powers or rulers or authorities; all things were created by Him and for Him. He is before all things, and in Him all things hold together. And He is the head of the body, the church; He is the beginning and the firstborn from among the dead, so that in everything He might have the supremacy. For God was pleased to have all His fullness dwell in Him, and through Him to reconcile to himself all things, whether things on earth or things in heaven, by making peace through His blood, shed on the cross."

* Who is this passage talking about?

* List everything He is or does.

♥ How does understanding Christ—who He was and what He did—help you grow in humility?

SPECIAL ♥ INVITATION

After each chapter of this study you have been reading a personal testimony from a post-abortive sister in Christ. Hopefully their stories and this study have been used by the Lord to bring healing in your own life. On this page, you are invited to share *your* own personal testimony of how God has worked. God bless you, beloved in the Lord.

SUMMARY

You've come to the end of this study and I truly hope it has been profitable for you. As you reflect back on your journey, can you see the changes in your thoughts, emotions and will that the Spirit brought about as you meditated upon and believed the Word of God? Have you experienced healing? May your thanksgiving overflow to the glory of God!

*Scripture: Psalm 147:1-11 Read this psalm out loud in worship.

Praise the Lord.
How good it is to sing praises to our God, how pleasant and fitting to praise Him!
The Lord builds up Jerusalem; He gathers the exiles of Israel.
He heals the brokenhearted and binds up their wounds.
He determines the number of the stars and calls them each by name.
Great is our Lord and mighty in power; His understanding has no limit.
The Lord sustains the humble but casts the wicked to the ground.
Sing to the Lord with thanksgiving; make music to our God on the harp.
He covers the sky with clouds;
He supplies the earth with rain and makes grass grow on the hills.
He provides food for the cattle and for the young ravens when they call.
His pleasure is not in the strength of the horse,
nor His delight in the legs of a man;
the Lord delights in those who fear Him,
who put their hope in His unfailing love.

NOTE TO GROUP LEADERS/FACILITATORS:

When I wrote this workbook, my focus was directed primarily to the individual woman who would be doing the study. However, women can certainly benefit greatly from being part of a group to discuss the material, pray for one another and provide accountability. If you have a burden to lead a group, may the Lord bless you! I do offer the following suggestions:

1) You must be a believer and you should do this Bible study before leading a group and in so doing study the Bible references contained therein and be prepared to answer questions. Are there any unresolved issues in your own life that need to be addressed? With God's help, address them!

2) Wait on the Lord. Bathe your decision to lead a group with prayer. Is this the Lord's timing?

3) In terms of format, you will notice that every day of each chapter, with the exception of Chapter 3, has two questions which can be used as group questions. One is a personal question preceded by the heart (♥) symbol. The other is a key question, preceded by a (↦) symbol.

4) You might also use group time as a time for prayer for each other. Individuals could check in with each other and support one another emotionally. Also, group time could be used for discussing any questions the women have. Group time could last anywhere from 1-2 hours.

5) You might want to set a time limit for prayer requests so that you have time to pray for each other. One suggestion to save time is to have each woman write out her prayer request on an index card and use the cards during prayer time. You could pray as a whole group or divide into smaller groups to pray more specifically for one another.

NOTE FOR THOSE UNSURE OF THEIR BELIEF:

If you are not a believer, then you certainly can become one today or at any point while doing this study. When I use the word "believer" I am referring to a person who believes in Jesus Christ and is trusting Him as her personal Savior. If you have not yet come to believe in Jesus Christ as your Lord and Savior; then I invite you to read the following Bible passages and pray to ask Jesus in to your life, today! The Scripture teaches that we have all sinned and are separated from God who is our Creator. *"For all have sinned and fall short of the glory of God,"* according to Romans 3:23 and, in Ephesians 4:17-18, we are told, *"So I tell you this, and insist on it in the Lord, that you must no longer live as the Gentiles do, in the futility of their thinking. They are darkened in their understanding and separated from the life of God because of the ignorance that is in them due to the hardening of their hearts."* From the Bible, we also learn that Jesus, the Son of God, came to earth, lived a sinless life, and willingly died in your place as payment for your sins; *"You see, at just the right time, when we were still powerless, Christ died for the ungodly. But God demonstrates His own love for us in this: While we were still sinners, Christ died for us."* Romans 5:6-8 Becoming a believer involves believing these Bible truths: by your own choice you have sinned; you deserve God's punishment for sin; and Jesus, who committed no sin, took God's punishment for your sin by dying on a cross. Genuine belief goes a step beyond believing these truths intellectually; they must be received personally and confessed to God. In *Romans 10: 9-11*, God tells us: *"That if you confess with your mouth, 'Jesus is Lord,' and believe in your heart that God raised Him from the dead, you will be saved. For it is with your heart that you believe and are justified, and it is with your mouth that you confess and are saved. As the Scripture says, 'Anyone who trusts in Him will never be put to shame.' "* Following is a prayer you can pray to receive Jesus Christ as your Savior:

Heavenly Father:
I come to you in prayer asking for the forgiveness of
my sins. I confess with my mouth and believe with my
heart that Jesus is your Son, and that He died on the
cross at Calvary that I might be forgiven and have
eternal life in the Kingdom of Heaven. Father, I believe
that Jesus rose from the dead and I ask You right now
to come in to my life and be my personal Lord and
Savior. I repent of my sins and surrender my life to You.
I thank you for Your saving grace which makes me your child
now and for eternity. In Jesus' Name, Amen.

If you prayed that prayer or one similar with a sincere heart, then you can be assured that you are forgiven your sins and have eternal life with God. *I John 5:12-13* states: *"He who has the Son has life; he who does not have the Son of God does not have life. I write these things to you who believe in the Name of the Son of God so that you may know that you have eternal life."*

ENDNOTES

Chapter 5, Day 2

C.J. Mahaney, *The Cross Centered Life* (Colorado Springs, CO: Multnomah Books, 2002), 39.

Chapter 7, Day 1

Dr. Tim Keller, Pastor of Redeemer Presbyterian Church in Manhattan, NY.

Chapter 8, Day 2

Jay Adams, *The Christian Counselor's Manual* (Grand Rapids, MI: Zondervan), 65.

Deb's testimony

Roy Hession, *The Calvary Road*